BLOODY B
HISTO

NORWICH

BLOODY BRITISH HISTORY

HISTORY

NORWICH

MARK MOWER

First published in 2014

The History Press
The Mill, Brimscombe Port
Stroud, Gloucestershire, GL5 2QG
www.thehistorypress.co.uk

British Library Cataloguing in Publication Data.
A catalogue record for this book is available from the British Library.

ISBN 978 0 7524 7658 2

Typesetting and origination by The History Press
Printed in Great Britain

CONTENTS

INTRODUCTION AND ACKNOWLEDGEMENTS

NORWICH IS INDEED a fine and remarkable city. In George Borrow's 1851 novel *Lavengro*, the character Jasper Petulengro stands on Mousehold Heath and reflects on the vista before him:

A fine old city, truly, is that, view it from whatever side you will; but it shows best from the east, where the ground, bold and elevated, overlooks the fair and fertile valley in which it stands. Gazing from those heights, the eye beholds a scene which cannot fail to awaken, even in the least sensitive bosom, feelings of pleasure and admiration.

In the thousand years of its history as an inhabited community, little has diminished that panoramic and uplifting view of Norwich. And through all of the crises and challenges of English history, it has shown itself to be resilient – from Viking torchbearers to Nazi incendiaries, the city has not only survived, but has continued to flourish.

Norwich is the largest walled medieval city in England and has the greatest number of medieval churches in Northern Europe. Following a riot in 1274, it had the dubious distinction of being the only city to have its citizens excommunicated by a Pope – a general absolution came from Rome two years later, when the spat between the clergy and city-dwellers was finally resolved.

Norwich is often noted for its pioneering and radical history. It launched the first English provincial newspaper in 1701 and was the first location in the UK to have a postcode. Its council was also the first local authority in the country to install a computer.

It would be wrong to suggest, however, that Norwich has not had its darker moments – periods of history defined more by grisly deaths, grim diseases and gruesome destruction than any of its more positive achievements. In this climate has festered religious intolerance, murderous intent and lusts for power that might be said to have tarnished the city's reputation as a sophisticated, enlightened and urbane conurbation.

Such, then, is the nature of this condensed volume. It does not pretend to be a comprehensive or overly academic account of Norwich's past. The English

The view from Mousehold Heath in 1818.

historian Edward Gibbon once suggested that: 'History is indeed little more than the register of the crimes, follies and misfortunes of mankind.' If that is the case, this book can be said to present a fair slice of the city's history, without all of the long-winded passages of an educational text. Either way, I hope that my lasting affection for the city's past comes through loud and clear.

A number of people helped me in researching and writing this book and I would like to express my thanks to the following for their kind assistance and invaluable support: Jonathan Plunkett, for use of some of the marvellous photographs of old Norwich taken by his father in the early part of the twentieth century; Clare Everitt, Picture Norfolk Administrator, for providing me with access to some of the unique images contained in Norfolk County Council's online database; and staff of the Norfolk Public Record Office of the Norwich Millennium Library for their knowledge and guidance on aspects of the research. Those photographs and illustrations that appear in the book uncredited are from my own camera or collection.

Finally, I would like to thank my wife Jacqueline and daughter Rosie for their continued encouragement and support.

Mark Mower, 2014

1004

VIKING BLOODLUST

Norwich Plays Host to Migrant Warmongers

IN THE AFTERMATH of the Roman invasion of Britain, it was to be the Germanic tribes of the Angles, Saxons, Frisians and Jutes that became the lifeblood of the East Anglian population, colonising large areas, establishing new settlements and cultivating the land. In their wake, the Vikings brought further influences to the cultural diversity of the 'East Angles', but not without fierce hostility from the incumbent tribes. This turbulent period of British history would see Norwich experiencing both the highs and lows of what the Scandinavians had to offer.

PERIODIC VIKING RAIDS

The Vikings may have been peace-loving in their Scandinavian heartlands, but were one of many wandering tribes that were unable to curb their bloodlust when travelling overseas. In the late ninth century, the heathen warriors wreaked havoc on the Christian population of East Anglia, destroying churches and monasteries and levelling homes and villages.

Like earlier foreign invaders, the Norsemen from Sweden, Denmark and Norway used the easily navigable rivers like the Yare and Wensum to attack local settlements. And while the early raids were often isolated attacks by a single longship, larger Viking raids began in the year 866, the *Anglo-Saxon Chronicle* recording that: 'the same year came a large heathen army into

A Viking longship attacking England. (Victor R. Lambdin, from Viking Tales *by Jennie Hall, 1902)*

9

Viking warriors in battle. (Victor R. Lambdin, from Viking Tales *by Jennie Hall, 1902)*

England, and fixed their winter-quarters in East-Anglia, where they were soon horsed; and the inhabitants made peace with them.'

THE BLOODY VIKINGS

The peace was short-lived. As an independent kingdom, East Anglia was ruled at this time by the young King Edmund. He fought a brave, but ultimately unsuccessful, campaign to oust the invaders, who had consolidated their position in Thetford by the autumn of 869. Led by the fearsome Ivarr 'the Boneless', the large Viking army fought a pitched battle against Edmund's smaller band of followers, which left both sides with heavy losses but no immediate victory.

It is thought that King Edmund and his followers re-established their dishevelled army in the village of Hoxne in Suffolk, where they were later surrounded and slaughtered by the Norsemen. Edmund himself was taken prisoner and, when he refused to capitulate, Ivarr had his archers execute the Anglo-Saxon leader. Given the scarcity of historical records for the period, it is by no means certain that Hoxne was

the place where Edmund died, and some have suggested that Hellesdon, on the outskirts of Norwich, may really have been the place of his demise.

A PERIOD OF SETTLEMENT AND PROSPERITY

In the aftermath of the Treaty of Wedmore in 878, England experienced a period of relative peace for the next 100 years. Under the agreement between Alfred the Great of Wessex and King Guthrum of Denmark, the Vikings were able to share out the lands that they held in England – known as the Danelaw – which were still populated mainly by Anglo-Saxons. Guthrum also adopted the Christian faith.

It was during this time that the Scandinavian settlement of East Anglia began in earnest, with Vikings marrying into local Anglo-Saxon communities and becoming merchants, artisans and farmers in the rapidly growing and prosperous towns of Norfolk, Suffolk

A modern plaque in the Fishergate area of Norwich commemorating the death of St Edmund.

THE IMPACT OF THE VIKINGS – INVASION OR SETTLEMENT?

Much of what we know about the incursions and settlement of the Vikings in East Anglia comes from the *Anglo-Saxon Chronicle*. This is a collection of annals, written in Old English, which tell the history of the Anglo-Saxons. Although incomplete, the documents which have survived give us periodic glimpses into the remarkable story of the Norsemen from the ninth to the twelfth centuries.

We know that Vikings settled in Norwich, but physical evidence of their occupation is scant. There are no buildings surviving from the era, although modern excavations on the site of the Anglia TV studios did unearth the remains of a small Scandinavian timber church. That said, over the years there have been tantalising finds which hint at their residency: a Viking sword recovered from the River Wensum; bone combs, soapstone and metalwork from Norway; and a Scandinavian burial cross unearthed in Rose Lane.

There are no references to Norwich in the early part of the *Anglo-Saxon Chronicle*, although the name does appear on the silver coins of King Athelstan in the period 924 to 939 – suggesting that they were minted within the city. Many historians and archaeologists now believe that while the numbers of Vikings which settled in Norwich may have been relatively small, their economic and cultural impact was extremely significant. A glance at a Norwich map provides clear evidence of this, with street names like Colegate and Fishergate (from the Old Norse 'gata', meaning street) and Tombland ('tom' meaning the 'open land' used as a marketplace).

The Fishergate area of the city where the Vikings first settled.

and Essex. One of these was Norwich, which by the early ninth century had achieved the status of a large urban burgh – or fortified town – with strong trading connections across Europe. By the end of the Viking era, it would have a population of between 5,000 and 10,000 inhabitants, making it the fifth largest town in England.

The original Anglo-Saxon settlement north of the Wensum became a much larger conurbation under Viking control. The Tombland area of the modern city was also developed as the main administrative centre, housing the Earl's Palace and playing host to a weekly market.

THE SACKING OF THE CITY

England's period of relative peace came to an end in the late tenth century with the death of King Edgar. His 10-year-old son, Ethelred, succeeded to the throne in 978 and Viking raids along the coast of England began afresh, dominating his reign until 1013. In an early attempt to prevent further incursions by the Vikings, the young king agreed to pay them Danegeld – sums of money to secure the peace. It was an ultimately fruitless exercise that failed to prevent the attacks and which earned him his nickname 'Ethelred the Unready' (from 'un-raed', meaning 'lack of council').

Every year from 997 to 1014, England was besieged by Norse raiders, but it was in the year 1004 that Norwich felt the full force of the Vikings' savagery.

As part of an unsuccessful campaign to secure control of the country in 1002, Ethelred ordered a general massacre of the Danes living in England. One victim of the atrocities was the sister of King Swein of Denmark. Within a year, Swein 'Fork-Beard' raided south-west England to avenge his sibling's death and in 1004 returned again to invade East Anglia.

The *Anglo-Saxon Chronicle* records the attack on Norwich: 'This year came Sweyne with his fleet to Norwich, plundering and burning the whole town.' It was a decisive and devastating attack which razed the wooden and thatched buildings of the city to the ground. The Danish-born nobleman charged with defending Norfolk – Ealdorman (Earl) Ulfketel – sought to agree a truce with Swein in the days following the attack, but Swein was in no mood to relent. Three weeks later, his army attacked and burned Thetford.

THE LEGACY OF THE VIKINGS

By the time of its sacking, Norwich had replaced Thetford as the main trading centre of Viking Norfolk. With better access to the sea and a strong local economy, the city was also able to rebuild quickly and re-establish its dominance in the region. By the time of the Norman Conquest it had undergone something of a renaissance, just in time to greet the new influx of invaders.

1075

THE NORMAN REBELLION

NORWICH'S IMPOSING CASTLE has a long and turbulent past. Even in the early years of its construction, it was at the centre of the conflicts being played out between the ruling barons of the new Norman order. This erupted into a full-scale rebellion in 1075 while William the Conqueror was away from the country and back in his Normandy homelands. What followed was the last serious challenge to his rule as the first Norman king of England.

THE DECISION TO BUILD A CASTLE

When Edward the Confessor died without offspring in January 1066, it was clear that there would be trouble among England's ruling elite. With no clear heir to the throne, a number of claimants would emerge, at home and abroad, all intent on underlining their claim with violence if necessary. After pitched battles at Fulford, Stamford Bridge and Hastings – where the last Anglo-Saxon king of England was slain – it was Duke William of Normandy, better known to his contemporaries as 'William the Bastard', who finally took the throne in October 1066.

His coronation occurred later that year, on Christmas Day.

William the Conqueror's consolidation of power took some years to come to fruition. His initial concern was to crush the resistance of the Scots and secure the border between England and Scotland. This he completed in 1072, by invading Scotland and agreeing a truce with the Scottish king.

In England, William looked to build a network of castles to strengthen the Norman grip on power and establish fortresses for his trusted barons and those Saxon lords that could be trusted to operate in allegiance with the king.

Norwich was an obvious choice for one of the new Norman castles. It was now one of the largest cities in the country, where Norman control was substantial. Many of the wealthiest Saxon occupants had left or had seen their land ownership and status reduced. The Normans had also cleared a large swathe of Saxon homes in the city to enable the construction of both a castle and a new cathedral. The construction of the castle began in about 1067, with the earthworks required to create a timber fortification, surrounded by deep, defensive ditches. With its garrison of soldiers installed, the castle was at last defensible and

William the Conqueror.

Norwich looked to have become one of the strongholds of William's kingdom.

THE REBELLION KICKS OFF

The rebellion of 1075 was led by two prominent Norman barons and one of the last Saxon earls of England. For that reason it is often known as the 'Rebellion of the Three Earls'. The three were Roger de Breteuil (Earl of Hereford), Ralph Guader (Earl of East Anglia) and the Saxon Waltheof (Earl of Northumbria).

Ralph was the main protagonist in the East of England and was the son of Ralph the Staller, a French supporter of King Edward the Confessor. In 1069, he inherited his father's title of Earl of East Anglia and in the following year was

made Constable of Norwich Castle. In 1075 he married Emma, daughter of Earl William FitzOsbern (the previous constable of the castle, who died in 1071) and sister of Roger, Earl of Hereford.

The plans for the rebellion were formed during the wedding feast of Ralph and Emma in Exning (then in Cambridgeshire) at which the three earls were present. Ralph and Roger were disgruntled about the division of power and land under King William I's rule, having inherited only a proportion of what they believed their fathers had owned before them. They invited Waltheof to join them.

RALPH GUADER MAKES A STAND

While powerful allies, the warring earls led an ultimately unsuccessful campaign to unseat William, and were thwarted in their attempts to gain the support of other English nobles. As part of the rebellion they asked the Danes to send a fleet of ships to assist them, to which the Danes consented. In the event, while the ships were launched, they never landed in England.

Archbishop Lanfranc was regent for William while the king was absent in Normandy. It appears that the plotters were betrayed by Waltheof, who had reservations about the rebellion from the outset. He informed the archbishop about the earls' plans and Lanfranc was able to mobilise opposition to the rebellion from an early stage. Although Waltheof was eventually beheaded by William for his part in the rebellion, he was later venerated as 'Saint Waltheof'.

Roger de Breteuil's army mobilised in Herefordshire and was attacked and held at the River Severn by the combined forces of Bishop Wulfstan of Worcester, the Sheriff of Worcester and the Abbot of Evesham. For his part, Ralph attempted to lead the uprising in East Anglia and mobilised his soldiers to march from Norwich to join Roger. He found his way blocked by Archbishop Lanfranc's forces and, in a battle at his manor in Fawdon, near Cambridge, he was defeated by William of Warenne and Richard of Bienfait, both loyal to the king.

Ralph's bedraggled army retreated across his lands to the stronghold of Norwich Castle. Forces loyal to the king then laid siege to the fort, led by William of Warenne and Odo of Bayeux. Recognising that he was overwhelmed, Ralph fled the castle and managed to escape from England, making his way over to France and the security of his lands in Brittany. Behind him, in Norwich, he left his wife Emma to defend the castle.

EMMA MAKES A BETTER STAND

Emma proved to be an effective military leader, maintaining the discipline and morale of Ralph's soldiers and holding out against the forces besieging Norwich. From start to finish, the onslaught was to last for three long months. She also proved to be a skilful negotiator, ultimately striking a deal with Archbishop Lanfranc for a safe passage for herself, her retinue and soldiers to be reunited with Ralph in Brittany.

While the siege was underway, Roger de Breteuil's Herefordshire army was ultimately defeated and the rebellion finally crushed.

Norwich Castle, held by Emma after her husband fled to Brittany.

THE LASTING IMPACT

Lanfranc secured Norwich Castle with a garrison of 300 of his soldiers, effectively preventing any return by Ralph Guader. For their treachery, William seized the lands previously owned by the rebels and moved other nobles into the area to prevent any further revolts. He encouraged them to build further fortifications to protect East Anglia.

While stripped of his English lands, Ralph went on to prosper in Brittany, a region outside William's control. In 1076, he joined a Breton revolt against the king, achieving some military success. Years later he was to join other nobles in the First Crusade, surviving an often treacherous journey to fight in the Holy Land with his wife and sons. He eventually died before the fall of Jerusalem in July 1099.

A slightly later siege in action – this shows Crusaders, including William the Conqueror's son Robert Curthose, attacking Jerusalem in 1099. (Library of Congress, LC-USZ62-58245)

NORWICH CASTLE

Its Long and Dark History

THE CONSTRUCTION OF the stone keep of Norwich Castle began in 1094 under William the Conqueror's son Rufus (William II). However, it wasn't until 1121 that it was finally completed by another of William's sons, King Henry I (1100–35).

THE TURBULENT REIGN OF WILLIAM II

Rufus – known as 'William the Red' because of his ruddy complexion – acceded to the throne of England on the death of his father in 1087. His reign was to last just thirteen years and was a period defined more by turmoil than tranquillity. He spent much of his time trying to capture Normandy from his older brother, Robert Curthose, and faced rebellion from his own English barons as a result of the swingeing financial demands he made on his nobles and the Church.

To compound his problems, Malcolm III of Scotland twice invaded England during William II's reign before being defeated and killed at the Battle of Alnwick. There were also separate rebellions along the Welsh border and in Northumbria. William Rufus was eventually killed in 1100 by an arrow while on a hunting party in the New Forest, Hampshire. There is some evidence to suggest that this was no accident, and the throne was immediately seized by his younger brother, Henry I.

HENRY I COMES TO VISIT

While built as a royal palace, no Norman kings chose to live in Norwich Castle. However, records do show that Henry I visited the palace in 1104 and 1109 and celebrated Christmas there in 1121 – presumably to see the new stone-built fortifications. A year earlier, on 25 November 1120, he had been struck by a personal tragedy when William Adelin – his only son and legitimate heir – was drowned with the sinking of the *White Ship*, a vessel lost off the Normandy coast near Barfleur. William's death and the succession crisis it prompted led to a period of civil war in England known as 'the Anarchy'.

THE BIGOD REBELLION

In 1214, the castle was at the centre of a dispute between some rebellious barons and King John (1199–1216). His repressive rule and ruthless taxation of the nobles to fund a war in France had soured relations with the aristocracy and led to the 'Barons' War'. Roger Bigod, the Earl of Norfolk and Constable of Norwich Castle, sided with the rebels. In response, the king seized the castle from him and placed it in the hands of William Marshall, the Earl of Pembroke, and John FitzHerbert.

The rebels then approached Prince Louis – the French king's son – with a plan to help him become the King of England in 1216. John was forced to flee and eventually died of dysentery in Newark Castle in October. Louis' forces marched on Norwich, taking the castle and plundering the city. William Beaumont was installed as constable, but the following year, when Louis was forced to return to France, the castle was repossessed by Hubert de Burgh. With the accession of King Henry III and reconciliation with the barons, Roger Bigod was reinstated as Constable of Norwich ahead of his death in 1221.

THE MILITARY STRONGHOLD BECOMES A PRISON

The castle retained its status as a military garrison until the fourteenth century, when its importance declined. From that point, it began to be used as a holding place for prisoners and in 1792 was remodelled – inside and out – by architect John Sloane, to become a designated county gaol. It typically held less than 100 prisoners, a proportion of which were debtors, incarcerated for their inability to pay debts.

Despite its eighteenth-century improvements, the castle proved to be unsuitable and inadequate as a gaol. Between 1822 and 1827 a newly revamped facility was constructed on the site, with separate cells for the prisoners radiating from a central gaoler's house in the middle of the prison. This enabled prison officers to observe all areas of the cells and exercise yard. Tunnels were also constructed from the Shirehall to the castle to enable prisoners to be transported directly to the cells. By then, the gaol could accommodate around 250 inmates. The building continued to serve as a gaol until 1894, when it was turned into a museum.

THE CASTLE AS A PLACE OF EXECUTION

As well as serving as a gaol, the castle has a grim history as a place of execution and played host to a number of judicial hangings. Some notable examples are given below:

James Blomfield Rush – a tenant farmer executed for murder on Saturday, 21 April 1849. With his accomplice Emily Sandford, Rush had attempted unsuccessfully to defraud Isaac Jermy, his mortgage holder, who was also a county magistrate and the Recorder of Norwich. Jermy foreclosed on Rush, who paid the magistrate back by murdering him and his son at Jermy's home, Stanfield Hall. The public hanging of

THE CONSTRUCTION OF NORWICH CASTLE

Norwich Castle was originally built of wood and its construction is believed to have been started in 1067. The first keep was an earth and timber fortification and consisted of a wooden tower on a small mound or 'motte'. The materials employed enabled it to be erected quickly. The motte was created by digging an outer rim of defensive ditches and piling the extracted earth into the centre. While straightforward in its construction, the fortification was sufficient to withstand the three-month siege of Norwich during the Rebellion of the Three Earls.

The castle bailey covered a much wider area and its construction required the destruction of at least ninety-eight houses and two churches. The construction of a stone keep for the castle was eventually started in 1094 by William I's son, Rufus.

Rush took place just outside the castle and attracted a crowd of 12,000 people.

Hubbard Lingley – the last person to be publicly executed in the castle. The 22 year old was hanged on Monday, 26 August 1867 for the murder of his uncle Benjamin Black in Barton Bendish.

Robert Goodale – was sentenced to be hanged on Monday, 30 November 1885 by public executioner James Berry. Goodale had murdered his wife Bathsheba in Walsoken. He was well built, but lost considerable weight during his trial and incarceration, causing Berry to ponder how long both the rope and the 'drop' should be for the hanging. Having calculated the latter at 7ft 8in, Berry decided at the last moment to reduce this to 5ft 9in. The execution resulted in the complete decapitation of Goodale – the noose severing his head.

George Harmer – the last man to be executed in the castle. Harmer had been released from the gaol on 14 August 1886. Only a few days later, he was arrested for the murder of carpenter Henry Last and confessed to the killing (later retracting the confession at his trial). He was hanged on Monday, 13 December 1886.

Panoramic view of the city from the battlements of the castle.

Above Henry I, mourning the death of his son William Adelin.

Right Waxwork model of a Norman soldier in the castle's keep.

Model depicting the interior of the castle's keep in the Norman period.

Above *Reconstruction of a scene from the medieval dungeons.*

Left *A holding cell in the dungeons. As many as twenty-five prisoners could be housed in these dank, insanitary and verminous conditions.*

Right *Reconstruction of a nineteenth-century prison cell within the city gaol.*

Above *Reconstruction showing a debtor housed in the city gaol. These individuals were incarcerated for their inability to pay debts.*

Left *When used as a place of execution, gallows were erected between the two entrance towers of the castle.*

INSTRUMENTS OF PUNISHMENT

Right *A scold's bridle, believed to have been used on scolding or adulterous women.*

Below *A gibbet iron, used to display the bodies of executed criminals.*

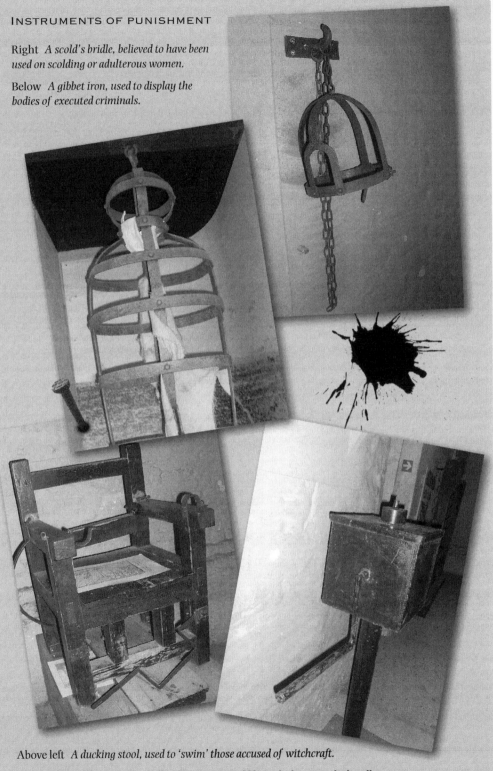

Above left *A ducking stool, used to 'swim' those accused of witchcraft.*

Above right *A prison cell 'crank'. A prisoner would be tasked to turn the handle a certain number of times to earn his/her food. The crank turned paddles in a box of sand.*

Clockwise from right

Death masks on display — these were used in the pseudo-science of phrenology which postulated that mental and criminal tendencies could be determined from the study of the physical characteristics of the skull.

Execution poster for a criminal hanged in Norwich Castle.

Reconstruction showing the imprisonment of murderer James Blomfield Rush.

THE
LAST DYING
Speech and Confeſſion,
OF
William Suffolk,

Who was executed this Day on the CASTLE-HILL, Norwich; For the moſt cruel and barbarous Murder of MARY BECK, (who is to be hung in Chains near where the Murder was done.)

1144

BOUND, TORTURED AND KILLED

William of Norwich and the 'Blood Libel'

IF EVER THERE was a local murder that could be said to have had enduring and international significance, it would be the rather murky tale of the slaying of a 12-year-old boy in early 1144. The death of 'William of Norwich' has resonated throughout the centuries, giving rise to anti-Semitic violence and hatred, based around the notion of Jewish ritual murder or 'blood libel' (the allegation that the blood of Christian children was used in Jewish ceremonies). But what were the circumstances surrounding this crime and the events that it gave rise to?

A BRUTAL MURDER – A TALL TALE

Like much of Norwich's history in the Early Middle Ages, the story behind the slaying of young William was recounted many years after the events were said to have taken place. In fact, Thomas of Monmouth – a monk from the Benedictine priory at Norwich – produced the account around 1170 and had come to the city some years after the murder. His book in Latin, *The Life and Miracles of* *St William of Norwich*, not only provided the first documented account of the crime, but helped to establish the cult of William as a Christian martyr.

According to the account, the murdered child was born on 2 February 1132 to parents Wenstan and Elviva. His father farmed locally and his mother was the daughter of a married priest. It is likely that the family lived at Haveringland, some 9 miles north-west of Norwich.

A portrait of William of Norwich in the church of St Peter and St Paul, Eye, Suffolk.

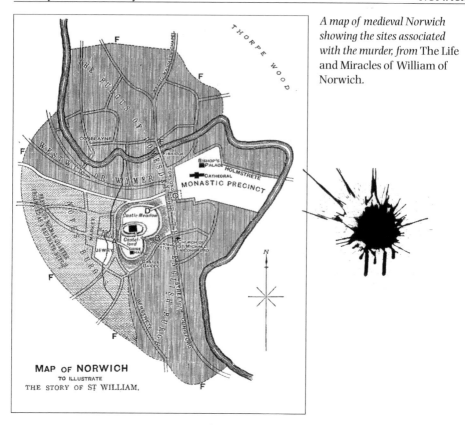

A map of medieval Norwich showing the sites associated with the murder, from The Life and Miracles of William of Norwich.

At 8 years of age, William was apprenticed to a skinner, or tanner, in Norwich and lodged with a man called Wulward. The pair were said to have frequent dealings with Jews living in the city, although both Wulward and William's uncle, Godwin Sturt – a local priest – had apparently forbidden the boy from making such visits.

On the Monday after Palm Sunday in 1144, William had apparently called on his mother in the company of a man who claimed to be a cook for the Archdeacon of Norwich. The cook was keen to offer William a job in his kitchen, but on the basis that the youngster began work immediately. William's mother was not keen on the arrangement but a small payment upfront seems to have sealed the deal.

William then returned to Norwich in the company of the cook, who Monmouth describes as an emissary of the Jews. The next day the pair visited an aunt of William's in Norwich, telling her all about the job offer. She seems to have been sufficiently dubious about the whole affair that, when they left, she asked her daughter to follow them and report back on where they went. According to the daughter's story, they were seen entering a house owned by a Jew. It was the last reported sighting of the boy.

Thomas of Monmouth then recounts the events leading up to the murder. He tells of how William spends the night with the Jews and is kindly treated and well fed. On the Wednesday, after their service in the synagogue, the Jews are described seizing the boy, inserting a gag into his mouth, binding him with cords, shaving his head and lacerating it with thorns. After a mock trial he is then bound and nailed to a makeshift wooden framework resembling a cross and bled to death.

In Monmouth's book, this then becomes the basis of the notion of Jewish ritual murder. He refers to information from a character called Theobald, a Jew who had apparently converted to Christianity and become a monk. Theobald is said to have claimed that on Good Friday the Jews had taken the dead body of William and left it on the heath near Thorpe Wood in Norwich. Theobald also claimed that the boy had been murdered to acquire his blood for the celebration of Passover, saying that this was a long-standing tradition among Jews. This was a fallacious allegation, completely at odds with the teachings of Judaism, and was to create centuries of ignorance and bloodshed.

THE AFTERMATH OF THE MURDER

It is generally accepted that a murder had taken place in Norwich at that time in 1144. On the morning of Easter Sunday, the dead body of a young boy had been discovered in the bushes on Mousehold Heath. He was clothed, although his head was shaved and covered in what looked like knife wounds. However, one of two women who first discovered the body had also seen crows land and peck at the head, which may have explained the lacerations.

The local landowner, Henry de Sprowston, was informed about the

discovery and took charge of the proceedings, burying the corpse where it lay (it was eventually reburied in the monk's cemetery at the cathedral). Various people visited the site, including Godwin Sturt, who briefly exhumed the body and confirmed that it was that of his nephew William.

Godwin Sturt then announced publicly that members of the Jewish community were responsible for the murder and summoned them to appear before the Synod. Justifiably uneasy about the allegations against them, the Jews sought the advice of the sheriff. He advised them not to appear. The bishop was also consulted and stated that the Church courts had no powers to act as Jews were protected by King Stephen.

Legal proceedings began against those deemed to be guilty of the crime – the accused being told that a peremptory sentence had been passed against them, meaning that if they did not appear, they would be found guilty in their absence.

In response to the hostility generated within the Christian population, Jewish citizens were housed for their own protection within the walls of Norwich Castle. However, this did not prevent a number of Jewish leaders from being murdered outside of the refuge.

The tensions on both sides were also heightened at the time because a money-lender by the name of Eleazar had been murdered by Sir Simon de Noyes. In pushing for the knight to be tried for the murder, the Jews were told that the case of the murdered 12 year old had to take precedence.

King Stephen eventually visited Norwich to hear the charges in the case of William's death. Probably as a result

The martyrdom of William of Norwich – a painted rood screen panel in Holy Trinity church, Loddon, Norfolk. (George Plunkett)

of the lack of any real evidence against the individuals concerned, he brought a halt to the proceedings and no further action was taken against anyone in relation to the crime.

THE LEGACY OF FEAR AND VIOLENCE

With the unrest that followed, the Jewish community was subject to periodic attacks. Some of this derived from the lack of stability at the time, which came as a result of the continuing conflict between King Stephen and his cousin Matilda.

The civil war that ensued began in 1135 when Henry I died without leaving a male heir. His nephew, Stephen of Blois, assumed the throne, supported by a number of barons who believed that England needed a male monarch. Those remaining loyal to Henry's daughter Matilda – the Empress Maud – fought a continuing military campaign against Stephen's rule.

As moneylenders in the period, the Jews were extremely important to the king, who used the money they could provide to circumvent the need to raise funds from his barons. He took various measures to protect them from persecution, leading his opponents during the civil war period to claim that he was in collusion with the Jews. In the case of the murdered boy William, many locals were to assert that the king had been bribed by the Jews to take no further action in the murder trial.

Thomas of Monmouth's account of the murder came at a time when there were continuing tensions with the Jewish community and a growing cult based around the martyrdom of 'William of Norwich' (although he was never formally canonised). In 1150, the boy's remains had been disinterred and housed within the Chapter House of Norwich Cathedral. A year later they were moved into the cathedral itself – a specific chapel being created in his memory in 1154.

Tales of the acts of healing that had occurred in the vicinity of William's shrine began to gain ground and brought pilgrims to the cathedral. Monmouth's account helped to further boost the campaign of veneration and brought further income to the church from those seeking miracles.

Outbreaks of anti-Semitism were to continue in Norwich for many years, including the massacre of large numbers of Jews in 1190. On 18 July 1290, King Edward I's Edict of Expulsion called for the removal of all Jews from England, estimated at that time to be a population of between 16,000 and 17,000 in total.

THE MYTH OF JEWISH RITUAL KILLINGS

Thomas of Monmouth's account of the death of William of Norwich signalled the start of a malicious campaign of rumour-mongering and violence that spread throughout Britain and other parts of Europe in the twelfth century and beyond. The so-called 'blood libel' was based on the assertion that Jews abducted and crucified Christian children as part of their rites linked to Passover. Alongside the few bigots willing to believe such tales, the myth was seized upon by many of those who resented the prosperity of the Jews under King Stephen and Henry II. Alongside accusations of ritual child murder in England, the myth was perpetuated in Northern France in 1171 when the Jewish community of Blois was burned to death. Despite papal pronouncements by both Pope Innocent IV in 1247 and Pope Gregory X in 1272, refuting the involvement of Jews in such ritual murders, the myth has been promulgated throughout the centuries to persecute Jews in numerous countries.

THE REPERCUSSIONS OF THE STORY

Thomas of Monmouth's tale about the murder of William is pernicious and based on little more than tittle-tattle. In support of his assertions, he cites testimony from a range of colourful characters: a Christian serving woman who claimed to have been present and witnessed the ritual killing through a chink in a door; a man who alleged that he challenged two Jews carrying a sack at the edge of Thorpe Wood; the daughter who had initially followed William to the house of a Jew.

Sadly, malicious tales of Jewish ritual killings were to continue throughout the Middles Ages and beyond. There were at least six other cults which grew from stories of young boys allegedly murdered by Jews, including Harold of Gloucester (1168), Robert of Bury (1181), and Hugh of Lincoln (1255). However, it was the tale surrounding the death of a Norwich lad in the early part of 1144 which marked the first such claim of ritual killing.

EVIDENCE OF JEWISH PERSECUTION IN NORWICH

Jewish communities have had a positive impact and influence on many aspects of the city's culture since the Early Middle Ages. The first Jewish settlers came from Rouen in Normandy and took up residence in Norwich from 1135, forming a close-knit community located in the area between the Market Place and Norwich Castle. In those early years, many became successful moneylenders at a time when Christians were forbidden from profiting from the charging of interest on loans. The loans provided by the Jews enabled the construction of many of Norwich's most significant early buildings, like the cathedral, Carrow Priory and Jurnet's House. The latter was owned by Isaac Jurnet, a Jewish moneylender and one of the richest men in Norwich, who had significant property holdings in the city and was a banker to the king (the property can still be seen on King Street).

Jurnet's House on King Street. (Image courtesy of Norfolk County Council Library and Information Service)

However, it is clear that the business success of Jewish citizens like Isaac Jurnet occasionally stirred resentment among other Norwich residents. Evidence of this can be seen in a cartoon from 1233, featured here, which is stored in The National Archives. Found on an exchequer roll listing the tax payments made by Jewish residents in Norwich, the cartoon illustrates the negative portrayal of the moneylenders at the time. Isaac Jurnet is depicted as acting like a king in league with the

Devil and the cartoon pokes fun at his best known and most disliked money collectors at the time – Mosse Mokke and his wife Abigail.

Further evidence of what is believed to be Jewish persecution came to light in 2004, during an excavation of a site in the centre of Norwich, ahead of the construction of the Chapelfield Shopping Centre. The physical remains of seventeen bodies were discovered at the bottom of a medieval well. Pictures taken at the time suggested that the bodies had been thrown down the well together, head first. The remains were examined using DNA analysis, carbon dating and bone chemical studies. Seven skeletons were successfully tested and five of them were found to have a DNA sequence suggesting that they were likely to be members of a single Jewish family.

The archaeologists and scientists leading the investigation concluded that the most plausible explanation was that the bodies were Jewish and that they had been murdered or forced to commit suicide as part of the persecution of the Jewish community in the twelfth century. In March 2013, the remains were given a Jewish ceremonial burial in Norwich in an historic event attended by 100 people from a number of faiths.

A negative portrayal of Jewish moneylenders in Norwich from a cartoon of 1233. (National Archives, Ref: E401/1565)

1349

DISEASE, DEATH AND DEVASTATION

A Plague on all your Houses

WHILE THE PRECISE date of its first appearance in Norwich remains unclear, outbreaks of the plague (or Black Death) began in earnest in 1349, with further epidemics at a local and national level until 1665. As part of a worldwide pandemic, the disease brought unimaginable suffering and death on a scale that the city had never experienced before. It was to have a lasting and indelible impact on the social, economic and religious life of Norwich throughout the period.

THE DISEASE TAKES HOLD

The Black Death – or bubonic plague – peaked in Europe between 1348 and 1350. It is widely believed to have started in Asia, with the disease being carried by fleas living on the backs of the black rats which infested the merchant ships travelling across the Mediterranean and Europe. Arriving in Britain in 1348, it would kill a third of the population within a decade.

It is estimated that more than 57,000 people had died of the plague in Norwich by 1355. Further outbreaks of the disease in 1362 and 1369 killed off more than a quarter of the population. At such times, those surviving the Black Death were overwhelmed by the demands of caring for the huge numbers of dead and dying around them. Graveyards were continually extended and during the worst outbreaks there were mass burials of bodies in specially commissioned pits. The stench of death and disease was everywhere.

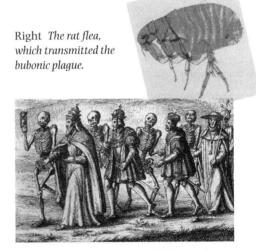

Right *The rat flea, which transmitted the bubonic plague.*

A grim portrayal of the bubonic plague which swept across Europe in the Middle Ages. (With kind permission of the Thomas Fisher Rare Book Library, University of Toronto)

THE IMPACT ON A PROSPEROUS CITY

It was during the reign of King Edward III that the bubonic plague first struck. Norfolk had grown prosperous as a result of the wool trade, with Norwich becoming the principal centre and main market for the production of worsted cloth – an industry that would thrive for the next 500 years. Within its walls, the city housed fifty-six churches, the construction of many of these funded by the wealth generated by local landowners.

By the start of the fourteenth century, the city's market area stretched from what is now London Street to Orford Place. It had been granted its surviving franchise in 1341, when Edward III visited Norwich as its defensive walls were being completed. This enabled the city to trade and to receive revenue without further royal permission. This cemented its status as one of the largest and richest settlements in the country with over 130 skilled occupations and trades and a thriving import trade.

As elsewhere, the plague hit Norwich hard in those early years. The rapidly declining population brought many industries to a halt and restrictions on travel made continued trading difficult. Coping with the large volume of sick and dying inhabitants became both a personal and public concern, the mass mortality leading many to see life as cheap and fleeting. Little wonder then that the regular outbreaks of plague were often a catalyst for increases in crime, popular revolts and bouts of religious persecution.

POPULAR REACTIONS TO THE PESTILENCE

For many, the coming of the Black Death was seen as a portent – divine retribution for the sins of man and the way that people lived their lives. Unable to understand why so many people were dying – and powerless to do anything to stop it – some were willing to believe that the plague was the result of everything from overeating and bad 'humours' to the clandestine activities of vampires.

Many with faith would carve the symbol of the cross on their doors with the words, 'Lord have mercy on us'. Prior to death, the Christian population became increasingly obsessed with the reading of their last rites. But prayers and supposition also gave way to more unorthodox rituals to cheat the Black Death. Some would walk around with

The Black Death peaked in Europe between 1348 and 1350.

THE BLACK DEATH – GRIM FACTS

The epidemic which swept Europe in the Middles Ages, killing an estimated 25 million people (possibly half the population at the time), is often known as the 'plague' or 'Black Death'. However, both terms were coined much later in history. Contemporary accounts often describe the coming of the disease simply as the 'pestilence'.

While it had been thought for many years that the outbreaks of the Black Death in Britain from 1348 were the result of bubonic plague, many scientists now believe that the huge death toll resulted from a combination of bubonic, pneumonic and septicaemic plagues. Either way, they were all pretty grim ways to die.

Bubonic plague is an infection that enters the skin as a result of the bites from rat fleas. Untreated, it kills two out of three infected humans within a week. Having entered the skin, the disease travels to the lymph nodes in the armpits, groin and neck areas, causing localised swelling known as buboes. The infected bacteria multiply rapidly and the disease produces a variety of other painful symptoms, such as gangrene, high fever, vomiting of blood, muscle cramps and seizures. The condition can also lead to a progressive series of other illnesses.

While less common, the plague can also be spread by the coughs of other people or through direct exposure to infected tissue or blood – giving rise to the pneumonic and septicaemic forms of the disease.

Victims of the Black Death being buried. (From the Book of Martyrs *by John Foxe)*

flowers to ward off the stench of the plague, which they believed carried the disease.

THE GREAT LEVELLER

The spread of the bubonic plague meant that no one was safe from infection, illness and death. Rich or poor, religious or nonspiritual, the disease did not differentiate.

Administering to the spiritual and caring needs of the sick and dying, a high proportion of clergymen in Norwich succumbed to the plague. Some parish churches – like those of St John Colegate, St Margaret Newbridge and St Matthew-at-Palace – fell into disuse as a result of the declining numbers of priests and parishioners and were closed.

However, the outbreak of disease also brought financial benefits to some of the religious orders, with wealthy patrons keen to buy their place in Heaven. Across England, there was also a thriving, but illegal, trade in second-hand monks' robes – the buyers believing that the wearing of these after death would fool the Devil.

THE CITY MAKES A COMEBACK

Over time, the plague turned many aspects of the established social order upside down. The rapid decline in the population meant that workers' wages began to rise and, in many rural areas, manorial estates were left without tenants and labourers to farm the land. Historians have often seen this as the main reason for the collapse of feudalism.

Compared to many towns and cities, Norwich was quick to recover from the rapid decline in its population brought about by the early outbreaks of plague. By 1377, the city's headcount had recovered to about 6,000. Many of these were peasants, migrating from the depopulated and unproductive rural estates of Norfolk in search of more lucrative employment and opportunities in the expanding textile industry.

With a clear sense of their own worth, these workers were to shape the social, political and economic landscape of Norwich as it continued to prosper throughout the medieval period. The new social freedoms brought about by the Black Death meant that these workers were becoming more confident in demanding their rights and questioning the elites that had governed them for so long. It would not be long before the peasants would start to revolt in and around Norwich.

1549

THE PEASANTS ARE REVOLTING!

IN THE AFTERMATH of the Black Death in the fourteenth century, the living and working conditions of many Norfolk peasants had actually improved. This was mainly as a result of the depleted workforce and the rise in wages which the labouring poor were able to demand from their employers. However, this relative prosperity was to be short-lived and cyclical, with periodic increases in unemployment and static wage levels alongside rising living costs in the two centuries that followed.

Having little power to prevent the broad social and economic changes which threatened their livelihood and existence, local peasants began to grow increasingly agitated and antipathetic towards the ruling elite. By the 1540s, this discontent had begun to fester in the rural towns and hamlets of Norfolk.

THE UNREST BEGINS

It was during a seemingly innocuous annual feast and Church festival at Wymondham, on 8 July 1549, that the simmering tensions between local landlords and the oppressed peasantry

who occupied their lands finally erupted into what was to become a bitter and bloody feud. The rebels took it upon themselves to make a stand and protest about the conditions they were being forced to endure. The peasants' leader was yeoman farmer Robert Kett, a local man who was determined to push the demands of the labouring poor and challenge the established order which had defined the operation and ownership of the Norfolk countryside since the Norman Conquest.

The peasants' grievances were many and varied, but central to their disgruntlement was the growth in sheep farming, which was leading to the enclosure of many common fields and the conversion of arable lands into pastures. As the land enclosures grew in number, labourers were pushed from the lands on which they made their living, with many being unable to provide for themselves and facing death by starvation.

In many respects, 57-year-old Robert Kett was an unlikely champion of the poor, but he was a man of principle and Christian conviction. As a well-heeled and well-respected landowner himself, he had taken steps to enclose his own fields. However, when a group of men arrived on the Monday after the annual feast to tear down the fences of his enclosures, Kett listened sympathetically and decided to take action in support of their grievances. He removed his own fences and rallied his family and local working men and women to stand up and do something about the untenable living and working conditions which many faced. In his speech he declared: 'You shall have me if you will, not only as a companion, but as a captain, and in the doing of so great a work before us, not only as a fellow, but for a general standard-bearer and chief ...'

AN AGRARIAN UPRISING

From this humble and essentially peaceful movement was to grow an agrarian uprising on a scale that had not been seen since the Peasants' Revolt of 1381. Kett mobilised his supporters and they set off the next day towards Norwich, pulling down enclosure fences as they went. At various intervals he gave addresses to the growing crowd, denouncing the landlords who profited from their labour.

When the mob reached the outskirts of Norwich, further fences were torn down and the crowd surged into the city. The mayor, Thomas Codd, was fearful that the protesters would burn and plunder the homes of the inhabitants and acceded to their immediate request. Leaving the city in the charge of his deputy, Augustine Steward, he agreed to take a list of their demands to King Henry VIII.

The demands of the protesters were revolutionary. Having established themselves in a camp on Mousehold Heath, Kett's entourage had drawn up a petition, which set out their grievances and the remedies they sought. This included the abolition of serfdom, an end to enclosure, reservation of common land for the poor and no further farming of sheep for commercial purposes. It was a direct and blatant challenge to the authority of the Church and the State. It could only end in bloodshed.

Elsewhere in East Anglia, similar rebel camps began to appear and the agrarian revolt began to spread.

THE VIRTUAL SIEGE OF NORWICH

In the camp on Mousehold Heath the peasant army had now grown to around 16,000. Kett was housed in a disused chapel and sought to maintain law and order and dispense justice from beneath a large oak tree. Many of his followers had begun to refer to him as the 'King of Norfolk and Suffolk'. Some of the gentry who were deemed to have been oppressive were rounded up and executed.

After royal efforts to end what was now seen as treason, the authorities in Norwich gave up on their attempts to broker a peaceful end to the rebellion and shut the city gates, preparing for further trouble.

Kett responded by bombarding the city with cannon from the lofty heights of the heath throughout the night of 21 July. The next day, thousands of rebels attacked and occupied the city for a short time until they realised that it would be impossible to defend.

The king responded to Kett's challenge by sending royal troops, bolstered by some Italian mercenaries with firearms; a force of some 1,500 men, led by the Marquis of Northampton and his deputy Lord Sheffield. A king's messenger had been sent to offer Robert Kett a royal pardon if he ended the virtual siege of the city. Kett's response was unequivocal: 'Kings are wont to pardon wicked men, not innocent and just men.'

Having arrived in Norwich, the king's forces set about trying to defend the city against any further incursions by the rebel army. On 1 August, Kett's men decided to take matters into their own hands. The city's defences were once again fired upon by Kett's artillery and the rebels made their way over Bishops Bridge and up into Tombland before they met any resistance. In the ensuing skirmish, Lord Sheffield was killed in Bishopsgate alongside other soldiers and Northampton was forced to withdraw from the city, leaving the rebels to set fire to some houses. It was a short-lived victory.

Modern plaque on Bishopgate where Lord Sheffield was killed.

Bishops Bridge, which Kett's rebels crossed to occupy the city on 1 August 1549.

THE KING RETALIATES

The royal response was a substantially increased army of 14,000 men which began to arrive in Norwich on 24 August 1549. This was led by the Earl of Warwick and included professional soldiers and cavalry with artillery, guns, pikes and swords. Over the coming days, their numbers were swelled with mercenaries from Wales, Germany and Spain.

What followed were several skirmishes across Norwich, with the rebels bombarding the city night and day and ransacking and torching buildings as they finally withdrew to their camp.

Having been entrenched on Mousehold Heath for over six weeks – with the inherent difficulties of keeping such a large force fed and watered – Kett took the decision to move his men and fight the royal army on open ground on 27 August. Some claim that the eventual encounter occurred close to the heath, while others believe the battle was

AN EARLIER UPRISING
– THE PEASANTS' REVOLT OF 1381

The Peasants' Revolt of 1381 was a significant attempt by the labouring and artisan classes to challenge the authority of the feudal lords under King Richard II to levy unfair poll taxes on all lay men and women over the age of 15. The poll tax of November 1380 was substantially greater than those of previous years and was hugely unpopular. When an overzealous tax collector in Essex was attacked in 1381, the revolt spread quickly to most parts of England, and a band of rebels led by Wat Tyler eventually marched on London to present their demands to the king.

As resistance to the tax collectors spread, rebels in Norfolk began to attack manor houses and religious buildings, ransacking them and destroying court rolls and manorial documents. Eventually, they besieged Norwich, forcing their way through the city gates, taking over the castle and plundering the surrounding area. The rebellion was eventually put down by Henry le Despenser – the Bishop of Norwich – whose large army defeated the rebels at the Battle of North Walsham in June 1381. While the Peasants' Revolt failed to overturn the established social order, it did bring an end to the imposition of the poll tax in medieval England.

fought in what is now the Dussindale area of the city.

The fighting proved to be more of a bloodbath than a battle. Robert Kett may have been a popular leader, but had no military expertise and could not draw on the resources available to Warwick. The latter had advanced through Norwich, hanging the rebels and showing little mercy.

Throughout the afternoon there were losses on both sides, but while Warwick's casualties numbered around 200 men, as many as 3,000 rebels were cut to the ground. Kett was helped to escape from the battlefield and rode out of Norwich to hide in a barn at Swannington. He was eventually tracked down by the king's

All that remains: the tomb of the famous Robert Dudley, Earl of Warwick. (With kind permission of the Thomas Fisher Rare Book Library, University of Toronto)

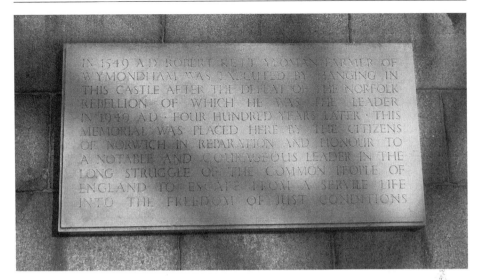

Commemorative plaque outside Norwich Castle.

men the next morning and arrested, to face trial alongside his brother William. The revolt was effectively brought to an end.

The Kett brothers were taken to the capital and imprisoned in the Tower of London. They were charged, found guilty of treason and sentenced to be hanged, drawn and quartered in the prison.

However, on 1 December 1549, they were returned to Norfolk to be executed. Robert was hanged from the walls of Norwich Castle on 7 December, while his brother William was hanged at Wymondham Abbey the same day. A few other conspirators were also executed, although the vast majority of the surviving insurgents were pardoned by the king.

ROBERT KETT – CHAMPION OF THE PEOPLE

Viewed from a modern perspective, Robert Kett is portrayed more as a Robin Hood figure than a violent revolutionary. Most accounts of 'Kett's Rebellion' now position the central character as a champion of workers' rights in an age of acute poverty and biting class oppression. A plaque erected in 1949 at the entrance to Norwich Castle reflects this tone and includes the following: '... this memorial was placed here by citizens of Norwich in reparation and honour to a notable and courageous leader in the long struggle of the common people of England to escape from a servile life into the freedom of just conditions.'

1557

THE BURNING
OF CICELY ORMES

THE REIGN OF Queen Mary I (1553–58) saw the brief rein-statement of Catholicism as the official religion of England and the repeal of all the ecclesiastical legislation passed under her brother Edward VI. Protestants who were not reconciled or converted to the Catholic faith now faced exile or punishment under new laws, and hundreds of dissenters of all kinds were executed, earning the monarch the sobriquet 'Bloody Mary'.

In what became known as the 'Marian Persecutions', those suspected of heresy against the Catholic faith were tried in open court and – where found guilty – handed over to the secular author-ities for punishment. The trials were conducted under the direction of the Privy Council, and with the approval of Parliament. The aim was to enforce religious uniformity and restore England to 'papal obedience'.

From January 1555, the country could legally punish those judged guilty of heresy and the adopted punishment for all who ultimately refused to recant became burning at the stake. This method of execution had been used by the Spanish Inquisition in the reign of Mary's husband Philip.

Norwich saw its share of religious intolerance and persecution in the period and the execution of heretics took place beyond the city's walls, in a large chalk pit set within Thorpe Wood and owned by the Bishops of Norwich. Known locally as 'Lollards' Pit' and lying close to Bishopgate at the bottom of Gas Hill, the area had been an execution site for at least 130 years.

The best known execution in Lollards' Pit was that of Thomas Bilney – a Norfolk-born preacher – who was

Early engraving of Bishops Bridge, which prisoners were led over to be executed in Lollards' Pit nearby, and (above) a modern plaque at the site of Lollards' Pit in Norwich.

LOLLARDS' PIT

The Lollards were a religious movement that influenced the early thinking of the English Reformation and the establishment of the Protestant faith. Their beliefs were based on the ideas of John Wycliffe (1330–84), a medieval religious reformer and the first person to translate the Bible into English. The early Lollards – or 'poor priests' – challenged many of the practices and beliefs of the established church and demanded social reform. They believed that the Bible should be available for everyone to read and the priesthood open to all believers. As a result, many faced persecution for what was seen as heresy.

Lollardism appears to have had gained some ground in Norfolk and the records of the Norwich Heresy Trials (1428–31) name those who were tried for this offense and punished in the city for their beliefs. This included several women, such as Hawisia Mone and Margery Baxter.

Old prints of the city frequently describe Lollards' Pit as a place where executions took place and author George Borrow, writing about Norwich, observed in the nineteenth century that, '... many a saint of God has breathed his last beneath that white precipice, midst flame and pitch ...' The area was originally the site of older chalk workings and lime kilns and, situated low in a valley surrounded by rising ground, had the feel of a natural amphitheatre – perfect for the spectacle of a public execution.

The area was eventually built over and today the Lollards Pit public house stands on the execution site. A plaque on its wall records the gruesome history of the pit.

The Lollards Pit public house, which now sits on the execution site.

---

convicted of heresy and burned at the stake on 17 August 1531.

In 1557, the infamy of the pit continued with the burning of Cicely Ormes, the 32-year-old wife of an artisan weaver from the St Lawrence parish of the city.

PERSECUTION IN THE CITY

As other chapters in this book demonstrate, Norwich has a long history of religious persecution. Just how many heretics were burned at the stake in Lollards' Pit remains unclear, although surviving records show that there were at least three such executions between 1428 and 1431. These occurred during the infamous 'Norwich Heresy Trials', in which sixty men and women were prosecuted for heresy in the diocese of Norwich. There were also a handful of burnings there in the early part of the sixteenth century.

It was in the reign of Mary I, however, that the persecution became endemic, with as many as fifty executions for heresy in Norwich alone. Those enforcing Marian policies – John Hopton, the Bishop of Norwich, and his 'bloody chancellor', Michael Dunning – are cited in John Foxe's *Book of Martyrs* as being responsible for the burning of thirty-one heretics. Foxe describes some of these executions, including that of Cicely Ormes. Like her, many of those who faced death were not preachers or clergymen, but ordinary working folk.

CARELESS TALK

Cicely Ormes was born in East Dereham, the daughter of Thomas Haund, a local tailor. Her grisly demise resulted from the execution of two other heretics in July 1557. Simon Miller from King's Lynn and Elizabeth Cooper, the wife of a local pewterer, were being marched across Bishops Bridge to meet their fate at Lollards' Pit. Watching the procession, Ormes was overheard pledging her support for the pair and was promptly arrested and taken before a local magistrate.

Despite suggestions that she had shown some contrition for her actions, Ormes was later taken before Chancellor Dunning on a charge of heresy. During her trial, Dunning offered to release the young woman if she agreed to go to church and keep her beliefs to herself. Ormes refused to comply and was sentenced to death. Foxe's account of her examination suggests that Dunning was loath to condemn her, seeing her simply as an ignorant, uneducated and foolish woman. However, having passed judgement, he handed her over to the sheriffs of the city, who held her at the Guildhall until the day of her execution.

Cicely Ormes was burned at the stake in Lollards' Pit on 23 September 1557, sometime between seven and eight o'clock in the morning. The execution was witnessed by a crowd of around 200 people. Later accounts suggest that she knelt down and prayed at the stake before making a speech in support of her faith and imploring the crowd to pray for her. The sheriff's men then bound her and kindled the fire which took her life.

THE MARTYRDOM OF CICELEY ORMES

Like other condemned heretics of the period, Cicely Ormes has been venerated as a 'Marian Martyr'. Her suffering at the hands of both the ecclesiastical and secular authorities testifies to the barbarity of a city gripped by the fervour of religious intolerance and persecution.

A depiction of the execution of Cicely Ormes in 1557. (From the Book of Martyrs *by John Foxe)*

1645

'THOU SHALT NOT SUFFER A WITCH TO LIVE'

LIKE OTHER PARTS of East Anglia, Norwich has a long history and tradition of paganism, folk magic and herbalism. It has also been the scene of a number of witch-hunts and witch trials throughout the centuries, many of which resulted from official misunderstanding and hysteria about these alternative beliefs and country practices. A significant number of innocent people suffered as a result of this religious bigotry and spiritual zeal, with the most significant number of witch trials occurring in the year 1645.

THE WITCH-HUNTS BEGIN

The Catholic Church first declared its official opposition to witchcraft in 1484, with a papal bull allowing for the 'correcting, imprisoning, punishing and chastising' of those guilty of 'incantations, charms and conjurings' and 'other abominable supersti-tions'. However, there are examples of the prosecution and punishment of suspected witches in Norfolk dating back to at least 1279. Nevertheless, it was not until 1563, with the collapse of Roman Catholicism in England, that the death penalty was prescribed for the first offence of anyone found guilty of using witchcraft. Witch-hunting in East Anglia began soon after.

The established church began to take action against many traditional Pagan folk practices like divination, curses, spells and magical healing, declaring them all to be evidence of witchcraft. And from 1604, with the backing of the Protestant King James I, witch-hunting was given added impetus when any attempt to cure illness by unauthorised means was declared to be witchcraft and therefore punishable by death.

In comparison with others parts of England, Norwich – and Norfolk more generally – appears to have had few witchcraft prosecutions in the early seventeenth century. One reason for this may have been the presence of Samuel Harsnett, the Bishop of Norwich, from 1619 to 1628. As a prominent writer on religious affairs and a future Arch-bishop of York, he was noted for his sceptical attitude towards witchcraft, which may have contributed to the relative absence of local witch-hunts at the time.

THE TREATMENT OF ALLEGED WITCHES

The legal process of pursuing witches appeared to be heavily centred on the Biblical dictum, 'thou shalt not suffer a witch to live'. Scapegoats were sought and anyone deemed to be unusual or out of step with the established community could be singled out for persecution. As a result, cases were brought against midwives, folk magicians, assertive women and disabled people. Even something as straightforward as a birthmark could be construed as evidence of 'the Devil's mark'.

Most alleged witches were poor, older women. Many underwent torture using barbaric practices like 'pilnie-winks' (thumb screws) and metal 'caspie-claws' (heated leg irons) to extract a 'confession'. It was little wonder that so many confessions contained strange and unbelievable claims of supernatural practice. It was only by confessing that victims were spared further torment.

The most bizarre test of a witch's guilt was the practice of 'swimming' or ducking in water. The theory was that water repelled servants of the Devil – if a witch or wizard floated in water, it was a sure sign of their guilt. Originally used as a general test for all crimes under English law, it became a popular – if unofficial – test for witch-craft for over 500 years. A plaque near Norwich's existing Fye Bridge (not the original structure) indicates that it was the site of a ducking stool used in the Middle Ages. This insidious device was used to punish 'strumpets and common scolds' and to test those suspected of witchcraft.

Plaque near Fye Bridge – the site of a ducking stool used in the Middle Ages.

WITCH MANIA REACHES NEW HEIGHTS

A more significant wave of local witch-hunting began in earnest in 1644 during the English Civil War, under the direction of Matthew Hopkins, the self-proclaimed 'Witch-Finder General'. Hopkins' reign of terror lasted until 1647, when he died of tuberculosis. By then, some 300 people had been tried and executed in East Anglia. The surviving accounts suggest that as many as forty people were tried at the assizes in Norwich as a result of Hopkins' employment there in 1645. Hopkins, of course, had a vested interest in pursuing all alleged offenders. He was paid a fee for every 'witch' he prosecuted.

After Hopkins, witch-hunting continued sporadically in Norfolk. In 1654, Christopher Hall was prosecuted for witchcraft at the county assizes in Norwich. Four years later, Mary Oliver was tried for the petty treason of bewitching her husband to death and was burned at the stake. She was one of only three women burned as witches in England – all of the others were hanged for their offences. Having executed her,

Above left Matthews Hopkins – the self-proclaimed 'Witch-Finder General'.

Above right The Salem Witch Trials. Bridget Bishop, the first woman to be executed for witchcraft, was born in England and married her first husband in Norwich. (Library of Congress, LC-USZ62-475)

the authorities sent an order to the city's gaoler for her possessions to be sold for the city's use.

The last official execution of a witch in England occurred in 1722, although it would be wrong to imagine that witch-hunts ceased at that point. In Norfolk, as elsewhere, local communities took it upon themselves to pursue people who they believed were responsible for sickness, death and disease and any unusual adversity experienced in the countryside.

NORWICH LINKS TO OTHER SIGNIFICANT WITCH TRIALS

Norwich has some interesting links to two of the most significant witch trials of the seventeenth century:

The Lowestoft Witch Trials (1662)
– two elderly widows – Rose Cullender and Amy Denny – faced trial at the Lent Assizes in Bury St Edmunds in March 1662, accused of bewitching a number of local children. Both were found guilty and hanged. Dr Thomas Browne, a celebrated physician, philosopher and author with a medical practice in the Tombland area of Norwich, gave evidence at the trial as an expert witness for the prosecution. He testified that, in his opinion, the children in the case had been bewitched.

The Salem Witch Trials (1692–93)
– a series of hearings and prosecutions of people accused of witchcraft took place in colonial Massachusetts between February 1692 and May 1693. These are known as the Salem Witch Trials and, of the seventy-two individuals accused and tried, the first to be executed for witchcraft was Bridget Bishop. She had been born in England and married the first of her three husbands, Samuel Wesselbe, in Norwich on 13 April 1660, at the church of St Mary in the Marsh. Her second husband, Thomas Oliver, whom she wed on 26 July 1666, also hailed from Norwich. Prior to the Salem Witch Trials, Bridget had been accused of bewitching him to death but was acquitted due to the lack of evidence against her.

1688

INGLORIOUS REVOLUTION

Anti-Catholic Persecution in Norwich

IT IS OFTEN said that this country's break with Rome – initiated by the Tudor King Henry VIII and resulting in the establishment of the Church of England in 1534 – was achieved without the full-scale resort to war and upheaval that was experienced in many other parts of Europe during the Reformation. However, while that may be true, it disguises the fact that the bitter religious schism between Protestants and Catholics was to continue in England until the end of the eighteenth century.

Much of this conflict resulted from the legal steps taken to outlaw all aspects of Catholicism, but the lawless violence of the mob in many parts of England also led to the significant destruction of life and property for those identified as adhering to their Catholic faith. Norfolk did not escape this religious perse-cution and Norwich itself experienced a number of anti-Catholic riots which had to be put down by military force.

The frontispiece to Thomas Cranmer's 1540 Bible, showing Henry VIII as the supreme head of the Church at the top, handing out the Word of God. (THP)

THE OFFICIAL PROHIBITION OF CATHOLICISM

The anti-Catholicism of the sixteenth century was drastic and far-reaching. The legal steps taken by Elizabeth I and her successors outlawed the religious practices of Catholics, preventing them from congregating and establishing fines for those who did not attend Anglican services.

THE PUNISHMENT OF CATHOLICS

—⊗⊗⊗—

Many Roman Catholics died in the years of persecution between 1534 and 1680. They were tried and executed under the country's treason laws. Pope Pius V issued a papal bull requiring all Catholics to oppose the English Crown as a matter of faith. The treason laws therefore made it illegal to be under the authority of the Pope and be a Roman Catholic or Jesuit, or to harbour a Catholic priest. The standard punishments for those found guilty condemned women to be burnt at the stake and men to be hanged, drawn and quartered.

The latter punishment was designed to be both shocking and ghastly, with the prisoner being cut up while still alive. After being suspended by the neck to the point of unconsciousness, the offender would be cut down and resuscitated. His genitals would then be cut off and shown to the watching crowd before being tossed into a fire. As if that were not enough, the guilty man would then be disemboweled using a windlass and have his arms and legs chopped off. The final humiliation was to behead the victim.

—⊗⊗⊗—

The Vatican responded by sending over to this country a number of English Jesuit emissaries, who secretly administered to the needs of the faithful and moved from one location to another, often protected and hidden by wealthier Catholic families in priest holes and hideaways, away from the gaze of the authorities. These Jesuits faced certain persecution if caught – an Act of 1584 had forbidden any English-born subject who had become a Roman Catholic priest since Elizabeth's accession to remain in England longer than forty days on pain of death. Those caught could be tried for treason, and hanged, drawn and quartered if found guilty.

Some of these Jesuits were from Norfolk and included Robert Southwell, who was born in Horsham St Faith in 1561. His family were part of the county's gentry. After becoming a prefect of studies in the English College of the Jesuits in Rome, Southwell was ordained as a priest in 1584. He volunteered to return to England in 1586 and moved around, serving the needs of many Catholic families until his arrest six years later. Tried on a charge of treason on 20 February 1595, he was hanged at Tyburn the following day. He is often remembered for his poetry, albeit that none of it was published until after his death.

ANTI-CATHOLIC RIOTS

By the early seventeenth century, Catholics had become an oppressed minority in England. Some historians have suggested that there may have been less than 1,000 in the whole of Norfolk at that time. Ironically, it was the bitter theological disputes between Anglicans and Puritans that enabled many to continue to practice their faith behind closed doors and without unwanted attention. However, this was not to last, with the descent into the English Civil War.

The Roman Catholic Cathedral on Earlham Road.

put William III on the throne with his wife Mary II, caused the most serious upsurge in anti-Catholic violence in Norwich. The city's pre-eminent citizen, Bishop William Lloyd, refused to take the oaths of allegiance to the new monarchs. This prompted a two-day period of lawlessness from 7 December that brought many hundreds out onto the streets and led to the destruction of city houses owned by Catholic families. The mob also attacked and destroyed a Catholic chapel in Blackfriars Yard.

THE EMANCIPATION OF CATHOLICS

The social and economic conditions created by the conflict led to significant riots in London and other urban centres – money was scarce, many found it difficult to work or trade and there were deserters on both sides looking to support themselves. In London, throughout 1647 and 1648, there were numerous disputes and demonstrations, while in the East there were lawless mobs in both Bury St Edmunds and Norwich. In the latter, the rioters shouted their support for King Charles and attempted to take over the city. The revolt was put down quickly and decisively.

The coup of 1688 – sometimes referred to as the 'Glorious Revolution' – that removed James II and

By the nineteenth century, the official persecution of Catholics had ceased and, as a prosperous and thriving city, Norwich saw its population of Catholics begin to grow significantly. In 1870, the city possessed two central Catholic churches and, between 1882 and 1910, work was undertaken on the new church of St John the Baptist, later to become the Roman Catholic Cathedral. This is located on Earlham Road on the site of the previous Norwich Gaol and was gifted to the city by Henry Fitzalan-Howard, the 15th Duke of Norfolk. It was designed by George Gilbert Scott, Junior and is today one of the best examples of Victorian Gothic architecture in the country.

1787

HENRY KABLE

The Convict Who Prospered

GIVEN THE HARSH conditions within the eighteenth-century gaol cells of Norwich Castle, it seems certain that few of the long-term inmates who resided there were likely to emerge from their incarceration in any fit state to thrive and prosper. However, that was exactly what one notable convict did. His remarkable story – set against the backdrop of Britain's punitive criminal justice system – has had far-reaching implications in the land that eventually became his home. Henry Kable may not be a household name in Norwich, but he has achieved a level of recognition in Australia as one of the 'First Fleeters' who sailed to establish a fresh colony in New South Wales in the spring of 1787.

CONVICTION AND CONFINEMENT

Henry Kable was born in 1763 in the small village of Laxfield, Suffolk, some 32 miles south of Norwich. He had an early introduction to crime and punishment, being convicted of burglary on 18 March 1783. Alongside his father, Henry Kable (often recorded as 'Cabell'), and a friend called Abraham Carman, the gang had broken into the house of a Mrs Hambling at Alburgh in South Norfolk. The *Norfolk Chronicle* reported their crime on 8 February:

> Last week some villains broke into the house of Mrs Hambling at Alburgh, near Harleston, in this county and during the absence of the family, who were in this city, stripped it of every

A waxwork model of convict Henry Kable incarcerated within a holding cell of the city gaol.

moveable, took the hangings from the bed-steads, and even the meat out of the pickle cases; it is supposed they also regaled themselves with wine, having left several empty bottles behind them. The marks of the feet of horses being seen in the orchard by a neighbour, was what first led to a discovery of the burglary.

The justice dispensed in the case was both swift and direct, and Baron Eyre – the trial judge at the Lent Assizes in Thetford – had no option but to sentence the guilty men to death. However, on behalf of all the prisoners convicted of capital offences in that session, he did petition the king for some leniency. In the event, while his friend and father were later hanged outside Norwich Castle before a crowd assembled in the Cattle Market, Henry Kable received a commutation of his sentence. He was kept in a holding cell within the castle to await transportation to America.

Transportation at that time was not a soft option. Convicts had been sent to the American colonies for some years to provide an alternative to execution. In many respects it was a convenient way to rid the country of its perceived criminal menace – literally placing convicts out of sight and out of mind. Those transported faced sentences of seven or fourteen years or a 'life' period. That time would be eked out working as an indentured servant, labouring under the most extreme physical conditions, often with the bare minimum of food, water and shelter. Many did not survive their sentence and it was rare that any convicts ever returned to Britain – the conditions of their transportation

provided only for a one-way passage and pardons were granted only in exceptional circumstances.

The colonists had rarely been enamoured of Britain's transportation policy and with the advent of the American War of Independence between 1775 and 1783, the ships had ceased to sail across the Atlantic. Until the authorities could decide what could be done with the many hundreds of criminals who had been sentenced to transportation, Henry Kable would continue to be housed in the holding cell at Norwich.

INCARCERATION AND ROMANCE

While the conditions of the gaol were undeniably tough and unsanitary, the castle did not operate like the single-cell, dedicated prisons of the following two centuries. Incarceration at that time was a more fluid affair, with communal gaol cells holding twenty or more prisoners at a time for a variety of offences. The gaolers made their living from the crowded cells, extracting money and other bribes from inmates and their families. Concerned local citizens and relatives of those imprisoned would often bring in food and other provisions to support the inmates. Male and female prisoners would also be housed together.

In this close-knit and unlikely environment, Henry Kable met his bride-to-be. Towards the end of 1783, 19-year-old Susannah Holmes, from the South Norfolk village of Thurlton, was admitted to the gaol having been found guilty of theft. She had been convicted and initially sentenced to death for stealing from the house of a Jabez Taylor. The items stolen included a variety of linen and some silver valued at over £2 – more than enough to secure a capital conviction at the time. However, like Henry, she too received a commutation of her sentence and was transferred to the castle to await the sailing of a prison ship.

In the bleak and unpromising conditions of their confinement, Henry and Susannah met, fell in love and managed to produce a child, which was born within the gaol in 1786. Henry asked for permission to marry Susannah, but this was declined by John Simpson, the turnkey of the gaol.

THE PASSAGE TO AUSTRALIA

In the same year that Henry's son was born, Britain had finally decided how best to solve its transportation problem. Plans were being made to ship 750 convicts to a new penal colony on the east coast of Australia – an area navigated by Captain Cook only seventeen years earlier. The Botany Bay colony in Sydney would be the first of many established in Australasia.

In order to provide some balance to the overwhelming number of male convicts being sent to the colony, the British Government took steps to transfer some of the female inmates housed in gaols like Norwich to the prison hulks at Plymouth, to await their passage to New South Wales. This included Susannah Holmes and her baby. Henry Kable's request to be allowed to marry his lover and be transported alongside her and Henry, his infant son, was again refused.

Turnkey John Simpson was obliged to accompany Susannah, the baby and two other female prisoners on the 325-mile coach journey to Plymouth that cold November. The drama continued at the dock, when the convicts were finally taken on board the ship awaiting its passage to Australia. On seeing the baby held by Susannah, Captain Arthur Phillip refused to take the child, saying that he had no authority to do so. Susannah was taken aboard alone, screaming and shouting, and placed in the cells below the deck of the ship, threatening to commit suicide.

Simpson, in a spirit of genuine humanitarian concern, took the baby off the ship and proceeded to take the first stagecoach to London to directly petition the Home Secretary, Lord Sydney, for some action in the case. When he reached the capital, he left the infant in the care of a woman who had also made the journey and met with Lord Sydney, persuading him to restore the child to its mother.

The public sympathies aroused by the affair finally brought some action to reunite Henry Senior with his lover and their son. In due course, Simpson was able to go back to Norwich with the news that the inmate would be allowed to marry and accompany his partner to Australia. He and Henry then made the return trip to Plymouth for the eagerly awaited sailing.

The media attention in the case also brought support from other quarters. A public petition led by a Mrs Jackson raised £20, which was used to purchase a box of provisions for the family to take

List of the female convicts on board the Friendship. Susannah's name is the sixth on the list. (State Library of New South Wales, item number 800179)

of supplies to sustain the creation of the new settlement. While disembarking from the ships in rowing boats at nearby Sydney Cove, it was Henry Kable who was the first to set foot ashore. Captain Phillip was to become the leader of the colony and the first Governor of New South Wales.

On the instructions of Lord Sydney, after whom the settlement would be named, Henry and Susannah were to be enabled to marry, alongside four other couples. The ceremony took place on 10 February 1788 – the first marriage service to be held in Australia.

Only a few months later, Henry was involved in a significantly different legal process. On the passage from England, the box of provisions promised the Kables and housed aboard the *Alexander* had been confiscated by Captain Duncan Sinclair. On 1 July, the Kables issued a writ through the new court of civil jurisdiction for the return of the package or compensation for the value of its contents. In the country's first civil action, the court found in Henry's favour and the defendant was obliged to pay Henry Kable the £15 he was deemed to be owed.

to the colony. This was loaded onto the ship *Alexander*, while Henry, Susannah and the baby embarked on the *Friendship*. The eleven ships making up the convoy – known since that time as the 'First Fleet' – finally set sail on 11 March 1787. When they reached the Cape of Good Hope, Susannah and young Henry were transferred to the ship *Charlotte* for the remainder of the passage to make way for some livestock. The journey was to take eight long months.

THE PENAL COLONY

The First Fleet had transported 600 male and 178 female convicts and some 200 marine guards to the anchor point at Botany Bay. The ships had also carried livestock and two years' worth

THRIVING AMONG 'UNPRINCIPLED ROGUES'

Living initially in tents, the prisoners set about constructing the buildings which would house the new settlers. However, it would be wrong to think that this was some idyllic convicts' paradise. The prisoners were set to hard work and the conditions proved to be unrelentingly tough given the new climate, soil conditions and limited supplies.

The British expectation that the colony would be able to speedily establish itself as a self-sustaining settlement with crops, livestock farming and fisheries proved to be ill-founded. Yet it did not stop the authorities from sending out subsequent waves of transported felons who were kept in check with the use of iron fetters and the lash or – in more extreme cases – a rope on the gallows. Captain William Bligh of the *Bounty*, the fourth governor of the colony, would later describe the transported prisoners of the penal settlement as 'unprincipled rogues'.

For Henry Kable, however, the new township provided ample opportunities for personal advancement. Under the watchful eye of Governor Phillip, he was given the task of overseer to his fellow prisoners. The tough redheaded prisoner proved to be good at keeping order and, in 1791, was made a constable and nightwatchman of the community. Three years later he was appointed chief constable. At the end of his fourteen-year sentence, he became an 'emancipist', one of the few transported felons who had served their term and were given the freedom to own land and set up in business. Henry took full advantage of the prospects this afforded.

KABLE THE ENTREPRENEUR AND FAMILY MAN

Henry's first commercial venture was to open a hotel called the Ramping Horse in 1798 from which ran a stage coach to Parramatta – another first in this land of opportunity. He next opened a retail store and then began to develop his land holdings, quickly extending his property portfolio to include half a dozen farms. In partnership with some fellow ex-convicts, he also began a number of maritime ventures involving whaling, sealing and the importation and exportation of various commodities like sandalwood. In doing so, he built up a sizeable fleet of twenty-five merchant vessels. All of this brought him considerable wealth and he enjoyed the luxury of a large house next to the gaol, which he ran as chief constable.

THE LEGACY OF HENRY KABLE

At a ceremony in 1968 to mark the 180th anniversary of the 'First Fleet', the numerous descendants of Henry and Susannah Kable met in Sydney to commemorate their status as heads of one of the country's founding families and to acknowledge their convict ancestry. Since that time there have been many other reunions in recognition of the important role played by the family in the development of modern-day Australia.

From his imprisonment within the straw-filled dungeons of Norwich Castle, Henry Kable's life was a remarkable 'rags to riches' story. A rare example of a convict who prospered.

In addition to the Norwich-born Henry, the Kables had ten further children, with all but one surviving into adulthood. One of the younger sons, John, was destined to become something of a celebrity, fighting as the boxer 'Young Kable' and achieving status as Australia's first bareknuckle fighting champion. Henry's daughter, Diana – after whom the first sloop built in the country was named – married the well-heeled William Littleton Guadry in 1809, seen at the time as the colony's first 'society' wedding. However, the family also had their tragedies, with Henry's mariner son James being killed that same year by Malay pirates in the Strait of Malacca.

BEFORE THE COURTS AND IMPRISONED ONCE MORE

Life in Australia had proved to be pretty good for ex-convict Henry Kable, but from 1802 he faced a series of disasters. In that year, he was dismissed from office as chief constable, having been found guilty of breaching Sydney port regulations by illicitly buying and importing pigs from a docked ship.

Six years later, and clearly still keen to flout customs regulations, Henry wrote (along with a business colleague) to Governor William Bligh to ask if the existing rules on the transhipment of goods from one vessel to another could be reformed so that shippers could avoid the payment of the dockside customs duty. Bligh was less than impressed by the tone of the missive, couched as it was in 'improper terms', and saw to it that both men were fined £100 and imprisoned within the gaol for a month.

In the years that followed, Henry's business ventures also began to unravel, with his various maritime partnerships being dissolved amidst a flurry of lawsuits. Many of these would not be settled until 1819. In 1811, possibly tiring of the pressures and problems of remaining in Sydney with such a high profile, Henry moved his family to Windsor, some 38 miles away, leaving his son Henry in charge of his residual business interests at the port.

THE FAMILY IN LATER LIFE

As a result of the move to Windsor, Henry senior opened both a store and a brewery in association with a new business partner. While his affluence and business success had been dented by the various debacles in Sydney, he remained comparatively wealthy by Australian standards.

Henry lost his ever-loyal wife Susannah on 6 November 1825 at the age of 63. He went on to survive her by some years, eventually passing away on 16 March 1846, aged 84. His eldest son, Henry, who never married, died six years later at the age of 66. All of the family were buried in a vault behind St Matthew's church in Windsor.

1797

FIRE!

Why the Blazes Does Norwich Love the Insurance Industry?

SINCE THE EARLY incendiarism of the Vikings, the history of Norwich has been blighted with periodic and devastating fires which have destroyed both the lives of the city's inhabitants and their property. Some of this has been the result of armed conflict, civil unrest or malicious damage. However, a significant number of major fires have started accidentally, spreading without warning and laying waste to sizeable areas of the city. Little wonder, then, that Norwich should have such a strong attachment to the fire insurance industry which thrived from the late eighteenth century.

MONASTIC CONFLAGRATIONS

Some of the earliest recorded blazes began within religious rather than secular buildings. Alongside the bouts of fire-starting in the Middle Ages – due to the often simmering tensions between the religious orders of the city and its lay inhabitants – some fires resulted from natural or accidental causes. On 4 May 1413, an inferno swept through the church and monastic buildings of the Dominican friars north of Colegate and spread rapidly to other parts of the city. Two of the friars died in the blaze and the damage was so extensive that it took until 1449 for the friars to return to their newly restored church and convent.

In 1463, the wooden spire of Norwich Cathedral was set ablaze by a lightning strike. As the structure burned, it collapsed through the timber roof of the nave, fanning the flames and consuming

Norwich Cathedral – a fire in 1463 destroyed the original wooden spire.

55

other parts of the building. The temperature of the fire was so fierce – estimated today to have been over 1,000°C – that it was sufficient to turn the original creamy-white stone of its construction to a fiery pink colour. Later modifications included the creation of both a stone spire and a fire-resistant stone vault.

WILDFIRES AND A WILD MAN

By 1500, Norwich had a population of around 10,000 and retained its status as one of the country's largest cities. Many of its Tudor buildings housed the prosperous merchants, artisans and officials that were contributing to its economic success. But these densely packed dwellings, with their combustible thatched roofs and timber-framed construction, were a constant fire risk, given the reliance on open fire cooking and heating.

In 1505, the city suffered a severe fire, and two more were to follow in 1507. These destroyed numerous streets, like those around the cobbled Elm Hill area, which today retains its medieval appearance from the reconstruction that was required at that time. The wildfires in March 1507 lasted for four days and razed 718 houses to the ground. Three months later, a further 360 dwellings were lost. In less than three years, around half of the city's housing stock had been destroyed and decisions were taken to ensure that the rebuilding included only homes with clay-tiled roofs.

There were periodic accidental fires for the next 300 years, with a major blaze in 1751 resulting in significant damage

to the tightly packed dwellings close to St Andrew's church in the city centre. Fire broke out in a furniture warehouse in the early hours of Tuesday, 22 October. It took no time at all for the overhanging timber buildings of Bridewell Alley to be engulfed in flames and the fire destroyed much of the Bridewell itself, at that time being used as a lock-up for prisoners and vagrants.

The turnkeys were forced to release the inmates, including a stocky middle-aged man with bushy black hair and a thick beard. It later transpired that this was 'Peter the Wild Boy' who, as a child, had been discovered around 1725 living feral and alone in the forests near Hanover. In later life he had toured Europe as a curiosity before falling into poverty and homelessness; circumstances which saw him imprisoned in Norwich for vagrancy. The sign of the existing Wild Man public house in Norwich commemorates his brief but eventful appearance in the city.

FIRE INSURANCE COMES TO NORWICH

The Norwich Union Society for Insuring against Loss by Fire was established on 1 March 1797. Its first policy was issued to Seth Wallace, a Norfolk blacksmith, and covered his house and shop against fire damage. From these humble beginnings, the insurance company has developed into the multinational corporation that is now known as Aviva.

The insurance business was significant, and not just for the financial cover it provided against personal and commercial losses arising from fire.

1797 – THE BIRTH OF FIRE INSURANCE IN NORWICH

From the issue of its first fire insurance policy on Christmas Day 1797, Norwich Union operated under a number of names, including the Union Fire Office and the Norwich Union Society for Insuring against Loss by Fire. Most often, it was known as the Norwich Union Fire Office.

In 1821, the company underwent a reorganisation and amalgamated with the Norwich General Assurance Company. In 1908, this was registered as a limited company, becoming the Norwich Union Fire Insurance Society Ltd. Between 1820 and 1962 the company's main offices were in Bignold House in Surrey Street.

As Aviva, the insurance group continues to have a major presence in Norwich and has contributed much to the social and economic development of the city in its 217-year history.

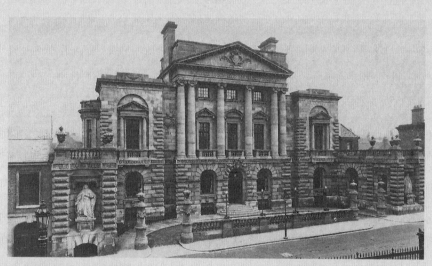

Bignold House in Surrey Street – headquarters of the original Norwich Union Life Insurance Society.

By 1821, Norwich Union had established twenty-five fire brigades in cities such as Norwich, London, Liverpool and Leeds. They were to have a significant impact in tackling fires and minimising the impact of fire damage. Over time, the insurance industry also prompted improvements in building control and fire safety, which enabled a greater shift towards fire prevention in Norwich.

BUT STILL THE FIRES CONTINUE

Despite these improvements, major fires arising from natural or accidental causes continued throughout the twentieth century and into the new millennium, leading to the devastation of some important buildings. On 31 March 1908, a great fire on the outskirts of Norwich saw the destruction of Lakenham Mill and the nearby Cock Inn, while a conflagration in June of the same year raised properties in the Aylsham Road area. A major blaze on the evening of 16 January 1913 gutted the Sextons boot factory in Fishergate. Overnight, a major part of the city's industrial heartland was turned into a wasteland. Other major losses due to accidental fires included Sprowston Postmill (1933), the Theatre Royal (1934) and Garlands department store (1970).

Perhaps the most overwhelming and symbolic destruction from fire – outside of the bombs dropped by the Luftwaffe in the Second World War (*see* p. 90) – came in the early hours of 1 August 1994, when flames ripped through the city's Central Library. This was the oldest public library in Britain, which had been in existence since its foundation in 1608. Norwich had in fact been the first city in the country to adopt the Library Act of the nineteenth century.

With more than sixty-five fire officers in attendance, the library fire burned for four hours, the smoke being seen up to 20 miles away. In its wake, the blaze destroyed thousands of historic documents and more than 100,000 books. Thousands of records stored in fireproof vaults in the basement also suffered from water damage as fire-fighters sought to extinguish the fire. The building was eventually demolished and replaced in November 2001 by The Forum – the city's state-of-the-art information centre, which cost £63.5 million to construct. Like a phoenix rising from the ashes, it has become central to the cultural identity of the city.

Right *A major city blaze in 1913 destroyed Sexton's boot factory in Fishergate.*

Below *The destruction caused by a fire in the Aylsham Road area on 22 June 1908. (Image courtesy of Norfolk County Council Library and Information Service)*

1823

A GRAVE CONCERN

Bodysnatching in Norwich

IN FEBRUARY 1823 two men were locked up in the city gaol, having been arrested on suspicion of grave robbing in a Norwich churchyard. Of course, bodysnatching was nothing new and the period between the 1740s and 1820s is often referred to as the 'Resurrection Era' or bodysnatchers' heyday. By then, everyone knew about the work of the resurrectionists, exhumers and 'sack-'em-up men.' But what lay behind this nefarious activity?

BODYSNATCHING – ITS GRIM HISTORY

Grave robbing for medical research has a long history, extending back to 1540 when Henry VIII granted a royal charter to the Company of Barber-Surgeons, allowing them to dismember the bodies of four executed criminals each year. From that time, the need to dissect the workings of the human body continued to grow, as did the shortage of research subjects. It was only a matter of time before inventive solutions would be found to this problem of supply and demand. From the late eighteenth century the gap was filled by

bodysnatchers, with Norfolk becoming a familiar hunting ground for these unscrupulous purveyors of human flesh.

One of the most prolific offenders was Thomas Vaughan, who was arrested in Suffolk along with two other men and brought to trial in Norwich for a string of grave-robbing offences. His punishment was only six months in prison. Technically, it was not illegal to disinter a body. As a corpse was deemed to belong to no one, logically it could not be stolen. The bodysnatchers were careful not to steal grave goods or coffins, so their punishment was often only a fine or a few months in gaol. With fresh corpses fetching as much as £10 each, this was a rewarding occupation with comparatively few risks.

A CASE OF SUPPLY AND DEMAND

The demand for fresh corpses came from teaching hospitals and medical schools, and it was the gallows that supplied the only legal supply of cadavers at that time. With doctors requiring around 500 bodies annually and executions

THE LAKENHAM BODYSNATCHING CASE

The oldest building in the Lakenham parish of Norwich is St John the Baptist and All Saints church. It has long been a historic landmark, although its relative isolation in the eighteenth century did present something of a problem – it became a well-known haunt for grave robbers or bodysnatchers.

On 13 February 1823, the recently buried body of Thomas Brundall was snatched from the churchyard. The culprits were Joseph Nicholas Collins and Thomas Crowe. They were arrested later that month and locked up in Norwich Gaol. Their trial at the Quarter Sessions in July revealed how they had operated as grave robbers and how they had been caught and charged for the exhumation. It transpired that they were in the habit of stealing bodies from local graveyards and transporting the corpses from the Rampant Horse Inn by coach to London in trunks measuring less than a yard long – each body being forced into the trunk by folding. Acting on some information received from London, a local magistrate had arranged for one of these trunks to be intercepted. It was found to contain the dead body of Brundall and so Collins and Crowe were duly detained.

When the lodgings of the two men were searched, the authorities discovered over a dozen skeleton keys which were subsequently found to open church doors in five locations, including that of the Lakenham church. Found guilty, both men were fined £50 and sentenced to spend a further three months in Norwich Gaol.

St John the Baptist and All Saints church, Lakenham – frequently targeted by the bodysnatchers. (George Plunkett)

delivering typically less than sixty, it was unprincipled surgeons who created this genuinely black market.

One of the best-connected surgeons was Sir Astley Paston Cooper of Guy's Hospital, who achieved considerable status and wealth for his unrivalled skill

Sir Astley Paston Cooper, leading London surgeon, who engaged the services of body-snatchers for his medical research. (NARA, image number 525430)

with the scalpel. As he later admitted, he owed much of his success to a lifelong relationship with a small, but proficient, band of grave robbers.

Born in 1768, Cooper was the son of a Norfolk clergyman. He was a surgeon to three successive monarchs, a doctor to the Duke of Wellington and served twice as president of the Royal College of Surgeons. In 1821, he was honoured with a baronetcy for removing a cyst from the scalp of King George IV. By that stage he was reputed to be earning £21,000 a year – around £1.5 million in today's money – making him easily the highest-paid surgeon of his time.

He spent many hours at the dissecting table and paid exhumers good money to deliver corpses to his back door. Like other leading surgeons, he acted as something of a patron to the exhumers, paying for any equipment they needed; providing legal representation if they ended up in court; paying their fines, and, ultimately, supporting the body-snatchers' families if any court cases resulted in their imprisonment.

On one occasion he paid his trusted bodysnatchers to disinter the body of a deceased gardener from the Heckingham Workhouse in Norfolk. Cooper had operated on the man's leg some eighteen years earlier and was keen to revisit his pioneering surgery. He had in fact arranged for the man to be tracked by local doctors in the years following the operation. In June 1826, the grave robbers completed their task without detection and transported the body by cart to London.

The surgeon wasted no time in dissecting the body. He discovered that his earlier surgery had resulted in the

growth of new blood vessels which had kept the patient alive for many years. Thrilled, he had the dissected leg mounted for display – it can still be seen at Guy's Hospital to this day.

THE RESURRECTION ERA

The apparent ease with which the body-snatchers plied their trade added greatly to the fears of local people. Norwich had several cases of resurrection in the early 1800s. In 1815, a watchman for the stables of the Duke's Palace Inn discovered three sacks containing corpses. It emerged that the bodies had been exhumed from a churchyard in nearby Hainford. The culprits were never caught and had been using the stables on the pretence that they were acting as apple merchants.

The panic caused by the growing number of body thefts led many Norfolk people to take action to prevent the graves of their loved ones being desecrated. In 1821, Mr J.M. Murray of Davey Place in Norwich was advertising in the local press the 'Bridgman's

Anti-bodysnatching device in an East Anglian churchyard.

patent iron coffins' that he had the exclusive rights to sell. History has not recorded whether these provided sufficient protection against any would-be grave robbers.

High iron railings and lockable gates were erected in some graveyards. Graves were often dug deeper than normal and nightwatchmen, sometimes accommodated in purpose-built watch houses, were occasionally employed by wealthier citizens to outwit the bodysnatchers. The thieves responded by raiding the graveyards of isolated communities that could not afford the more expensive security measures.

Ironically, it was the public fear of newly buried bodies being dug up and sold that strengthened the case for the first cemetery to be opened. Many believed that these could offer much better security against the grave robbers. The Rosary cemetery in Norwich was the first non-denominational cemetery to be opened in England. It was licensed for burials by the Bishop of Norwich in 1821, when the first interment took place.

THE END OF AN ERA

Over time, the insatiable demands of surgeons like Cooper were addressed through a more legitimate supply of corpses. New legislation allowed people to donate their bodies to medical research. The Anatomy Act of 1832 also provided for the bodies of unknown and unclaimed individuals to be dissected.

Cooper died in February 1841. He left clear instructions for his own corpse

Contemporary portraits of the bodysnatchers Bishop and Williams, with their accomplice James May.

to be medically examined before being entombed within a stone sarcophagus. He had little to fear from bodysnatchers.

The two trusted bodysnatchers that Cooper had commissioned to dig up the body from the Heckingham Workhouse in 1826 were less fortunate. John Bishop and Thomas Williams were arrested in the autumn of 1831 while attempting to sell the body of a young man to a London surgeon. They had despatched him in order to sell his corpse and were convicted and sentenced to death for what was known as 'The Italian Boy Murder'.

Both men were hanged at Newgate before a crowd of 30,000. Bishop died quickly, his neck broken by the drop. Williams suffered more, the noose eventually strangling him when his strength gave out. Fittingly, the bodies of both men were then taken away for dissection. That bodysnatching in areas like Norfolk had provided them with a good living was clear from Bishop's own words. Following his conviction, he confessed: 'I have followed the course of obtaining a livelihood as a bodysnatcher for twelve years and have obtained and sold I think from 500 to 1,000 bodies.'

1851

THE INCREDIBLE CONFESSION OF WILLIAM SHEWARD

IF THEY ARE concluded at all, most murder investigations are usually resolved one way or another within a few days, weeks or months of the fatal act being committed. Rarely do the processes of detection, investigation and criminal justice take nearly eighteen years to complete. Yet that was the situation in a bizarre case of homicide that bewildered the authorities in Norwich during the nineteenth century.

The resolution of this particularly gruesome crime occurred on the evening of New Year's Day 1868, when 57-year-old William Sheward walked into a police station at Walworth in London to declare that he had a confession. When asked by the inspector on duty about the nature of his disclosure, the man ventured, 'For wilfully murdering my first wife Martha at Norwich,' before adding, 'I have kept it for years. I can keep it no longer.' Distraught at what he was about to divulge, Sheward then wept and began to reveal, in stages, the strange facts surrounding the brutal murder of his spouse in 1851 and the cover-up that he had perpetrated since that time. Pieced together now, it is one of the most remarkable cases of murder in the bloody history of Norwich.

THE TAILOR COMMITS A MURDER

William Sheward had married his wife Martha Francis in Greenwich, London in 1836. She was 39 years old and he was some fifteen years younger. Born in Norwich, Martha had a brother and other relatives in the city and a twin sister who lived in Wymondham. Various accounts suggest that she was a short woman with a fair complexion and curly sandy-coloured hair, who had few friends outside of her family. History has also portrayed her as something of a scold and William as the put-upon and browbeaten husband. In reality, she was more likely to have been an assertive woman doing her best to cope with an introverted and socially inept husband who appeared to keep secrets from her.

Sheward was a tailor by trade and after the first few months of their marriage, the couple had moved to Norwich, where he tried his hand at various commercial ventures. In 1842 he was the licensee of the Rose Tavern in Ber Street and he later tried to set up a pawnbroking business in St Giles Street. When he was declared bankrupt in 1849, he resumed work as a tailor. At this time the couple were living in Tabernacle Street.

By his own confession, Sheward murdered his wife on Sunday, 15 June 1851. They had begun to quarrel at regular intervals, both publicly and in private, their arguments based around money concerns and William's apparent interest in other women. Martha had also threatened more than once that she would leave him. That morning, after a squabble about a trip to Great Yarmouth to collect some money from a Mr Christie, Sheward silenced his wife forever. His written confession contained the chilling line: 'I ran the razor into her throat.'

THE DISPOSAL OF THE BODY

Sheward's actions after the murder appear to have been both cold and calculating. Having committed the act, he covered the body with an apron and headed off to the planned meeting in Yarmouth. The next day he went to work as usual and returned home that evening. Noticing that the house had begun to take on a musty air, he made a fire in the bedroom and began to cut up the body.

At intervals over the days that followed, he took long walks around the city, disposing of various body parts in an effort to conceal his crime. He boiled the head of the corpse in a saucepan on the fire, broke up the flesh and bones and then scattered the remains around the Thorpe area of Norwich. Anything within the house that had evidence of blood on it was burned and similarly disposed of on his walks. Single-minded in his grim task, Sheward removed all traces of his butchered wife and set about concocting a suitable cover story for her disappearance.

THE COVER-UP

Martha's limited circle of friends and regular lack of communication with her own family made it easier for Sheward to claim that his wife had left him after one of their frequent domestic disputes. She had often threatened as much and Sheward maintained that he knew nothing of her whereabouts. Even when two of Martha's family passed away later that year and she was left some money, the family seemed not to be surprised that she had apparently vanished to some unknown location away from her tailor husband.

Sheward was also helped in his cover-up by the bungling of the authorities when the first reports began to emerge of human body parts being discovered in various parts of Norwich. On Saturday, 21 June, a dog being walked by a 12-year-old boy along a narrow path known as Miss Martineau's Lane sniffed out a piece of meat and faithfully carried the cut home to a property in Trowse. When retrieved from the canine's jaws, the dog's bounty was found to be a human hand. In the days and weeks that followed, the city police were besieged by honest citizens visiting the station house to hand in isolated cuts of flesh and bone that had been uncovered across Norwich.

THE BUNGLED ENQUIRY

After four weeks of searches and police enquiries, three local surgeons convened to examine the human remains that had been collected. All of the body parts – which now included flesh, muscle, hands, feet, leg bones and part of a pelvis – were scrutinised and the doctors determined that they were from a woman aged '16 to 26 years'. This was subsequently reported by the press and the public was asked to come forward with any information about missing women of that age. At 54 years of age at the time of her death, it was clear that few people – if they harboured any suspicions at all – were likely to believe that the missing Martha Sheward was the mysterious dismembered corpse.

Posters were placed around the city, stating clearly that body parts had been found and were being treated as evidence of a supposed murder (there had been a suggestion early on that this might have been evidence of dissection by mischievous medical students). The official pronouncement led to further body parts being discovered and leads on at least one young woman who had gone missing some time before. However, without a head, identification of the cadaver proved impossible and the enquiry ground to the halt.

Frustrated in their ability to identify the murder victim, the police scaled back their investigations and the body parts were preserved in dissection jars and housed in the lock-ups of the city gaol. In June 1856, the chief constable sought permission to bury the remains and a Sergeant Peck was given the unenviable task of interring the parts in a hole dug

The Guildhall, where the interred remains of Martha Sheward were buried for nearly eighteen years.

within a vault to the north side of the Guildhall. The area was then covered in a quantity of lime.

WILLIAM SHEWARD MOVES ON

Sheward lost no time in resuming his life, confident that he could get away with the murder. Only a year after the crime, he was cohabiting with another woman in a rented room in St George's. When the couple moved to the Shakespeare public house nearby, Charlotte Maria Buck became his common-law wife and in the years that followed they were to have five children. On 13 February 1862 they were married at the Norwich Register Office, with Sheward declaring his status as that of a 'widower.'

Fortune also seems to have smiled on Sheward's business life, and a new pawnbroking business set up in King Street proved to be successful. On 22 September 1868, he had sufficient funds to buy his own public house – the Key and Castle on Oak Street.

Above *The Shirehall, where William Sheward was tried in 1869 for the murder of his wife.*

Right *A depiction of William Sheward's execution.*

THE MURDERER REPENTS

Despite the passage of years, his apparent business success and new family circumstances, it was clear that William Sheward was a tortured soul. Reports would later confirm that he had taken to the bottle and would pace around at night unable to sleep, his nerves on edge. By the Christmas of 1868, he was consumed by his alcohol addiction and suicidal in his intent. In this distressed state he took a journey back to Walworth, where he had first met Martha Francis nearly eighteen years before. Unable to take his own life, he embarked on the next most logical step and arrived at Carter Street police station to confess his guilt.

Sheward's trial took place at the Norfolk Lent Assizes in the Shirehall on Monday, 29 March 1869. In the earlier magistrates' hearing, he had already withdrawn the written confession made at Walworth. What remained of his wife's body parts were exhumed from the vault of the Guildhall and two of the original three doctors who had carried out the earlier medical examination were called to give evidence.

Found guilty of murder, Sheward was sentenced to be hanged on 20 April within the walls of the city gaol. It was the first execution in Norwich to be held in private, away from the gaze of the public. On the day itself, some 2,000 people waited outside the prison gates

PRISONS IN THE CITY OF NORWICH

While Norwich Castle operated as the county gaol in Norfolk from the fourteenth century, the city gaol from 1597 to 1826 was housed in a building close to the Guildhall. In that final year, a purpose-built prison was opened near the gates of St Giles, close to what is now the site of the Roman Catholic Cathedral on Earlham Road.

The construction of the new prison required an Act of Parliament and the resulting building contained all of the features deemed to be necessary at the time, including an infirmary, tread wheels, debtors' wings, warm and cold baths, a laundry and iron doors with ventilation grills. Significantly, it was also designed to accommodate executions.

Norwich Gaol – a purpose-built prison that originally stood close to what is now the site of the Roman Catholic Cathedral on Earlham Road.

to witness the raising of the black flag in confirmation of his execution. He was later buried on the site.

The 'Tabernacle Street Murder' reads like a Victorian melodrama, although there was no lack of cause and effect in the eventual outcome of the story. William Sheward sowed the seeds of his own demise that fateful day in June 1851 in taking a razor to the throat of his first wife. His repentance proved to be a long-standing affliction.

1853

TERROR ON THE HIGHWAY

HIGHWAY ROBBERY HAS been a persistent threat to travellers since the dawn of time. Much is often made of the exploits of infamous robbers like Richard 'Dick' Turpin, but Norfolk also had its share of professional thieves and opportunistic footpads who preyed on the unfortunate along the highways and byways of the county. And while the authorities struggled to bring but a fraction of these felons to book, some did come within the full purview of the law.

THE HIGHWAY MENACE

One late example of terror on the highway came on Friday, 18 November 1853 and involved the robbery and murder of Lorenz Beha. He was a watchmaker and jewellery dealer who lived on St Stephen's Plain in Norwich. It was his custom to leave the business in the care of two assistants and travel across Norfolk on his rounds to gather orders and sell his merchandise.

Beha was a tempting target for highway robbers. He usually carried a box of gold and silver watches and other jewellery in a bag, suspended from a stick on his shoulder. He also pocketed quantities of money, having collected payments in small instalments from many of his existing customers.

About one o'clock that afternoon, a man called Robinson was walking towards the village of Wellingham, some 28 miles north-west of Norwich. Along the road he observed a large pool of blood and noticed that some of it had been partially covered by dirt scraped from the road. Within a short space of time, Robinson was joined by two young men who rode up on ponies and

Highway robbery – a persistent threat to travellers since the dawn of time.

two ladies who were travelling along the road in a horse-drawn gig.

Robinson followed the trail of blood through the hedge and saw with some horror that in a ditch close to some trees lay a body. Lorenz Beha had been dragged by his coat through a gap in the hedge and left for dead. His coat collar was turned up and beside him lay a box of jewellery – unopened, but removed from his bag – and a stick and umbrella. More sinisterly, a large woodman's axe also sat close to the corpse, the blade of which was covered with blood and hair. It was clear that this was the murder weapon.

When the men inspected the body at close quarters, they found that the man's trouser pockets had been turned out and rifled, although a pocket watch in his waistcoat was still present and giving good time. The head of the corpse was all but severed from the body by a blow at the back of the neck, and there were four deeply cut wounds across his temple and face. The right eye had also been driven inwards to the depth of nearly an inch. The attack had been both sustained and brutal.

On searching the clothes of the deceased, the men then found Beha's account book, again soaked with blood, and realised that the keys to the jewellery box were missing. It seemed quite clear that robbery had been the motive for the attack.

A SUSPECT IS ARRESTED

It took only a few hours for a murder suspect to be identified. William Webster came forward to tell a parish constable that he had been driving a cart from Tittleshall to Wellingham shortly before lunchtime that Friday, and had seen a man in the plantation adjoining the ditch where the body was found. He could not help but notice that the man stooped down and tried to hide on hearing the cart approach. He also recognised the man as being William Thompson, a woodman who lived locally with his father.

Thompson was taken from his bed that same night. Some of his clothes were found to be stained with blood and, secreted in different parts of his father's property, the police found two silver watches inscribed with the maker's name 'L Beha', a canvas bag with a third watch and money in notes, gold and silver. It was clear that the 21-year-old labourer had a case to answer.

THE JUDICIAL PROCESS

The following day, Thompson was taken before the county magistrates, who heard testimony from several witnesses and remanded him in custody until further evidence could be gathered. One newspaper account at the time described the prisoner's appearance as 'superior to that which is generally characteristic of his class. He listened attentively to the evidence, but appeared to be quite calm and unconcerned.' A few days later, the magistrates' hearing resumed and Thompson was committed for trial on a charge of 'wilful murder'.

At the Norfolk Lent Assizes on Thursday, 23 March 1854, the case against Thompson was clear cut and it appeared that he had done little to cover his tracks on the day of the murder. The jury heard that the woodman had communicated to his employer that he would not be at work on Friday, 18 November 1853, as he was ill. Nevertheless, that morning, he had been observed walking with his axe towards the plantation where the murder would later occur. The prosecution believed that Thompson had planned the robbery, knowing that Beha was travelling into Wellingham in the course of his business.

Thompson's actions after the murder similarly did little to disguise his guilt. One witness saw him walking from the wood close to the murder scene at some speed and without his axe. The man had stopped Thompson to ask him the time and the labourer had pulled a distinctive pocket watch from his waistcoat to assist. Two hours later, the accused was seen entering a shop in Tittleshall and paying a bill with 2½ sovereigns. The jury heard that his wage from the week before had been only 11 shillings.

THE TITTLESHALL MURDER.

At the Norwich assizes, last week, William Thompson, aged 21, was indicted for the wilful murder of Lorenz Beha, on the 18th of November last, at Tittleshall.

The unfortunate man whose death was the occasion of this charge resided at Norwich, where, with his nephew, he had carried on the business of a dealer in jewellery and watches, with which he used to make periodical rounds through that and the adjoining county. On Monday, the 14th of November, the old man started on a round through the northern part of the county, in the course of which he would pass through Wellingham and Tittleshall, at which latter village the prisoner lived with his father, working in the neighbouring plantations as a woodman and ditcher. On Thursday evening, the 17th, Lorenz Beha took two £5 notes in change, one of which was cut in halves, but had been joined by paper. On the following day, at half-past twelve, the deceased was seen in good health as usual, trudging along the road opposite a wood between Wellingham and Tittleshall, with his pack at his back and a stick in his hand. Near this very spot a traveller noticed, at half-past 1, a great pool of blood on the road, but he passed by. After this, at 3 o'clock, another traveller, more curious or idle than the first, observed the same pool, and, examining it, discovered a track of blood, and marks of something having been dragged from the pool to a gap in the hedge. Following this, he entered the wood, and in the ditch at his feet he discovered the body of the deceased, quite dead, and covered with blood, flowing from several deadly gashes on the head and face, either of which was sufficient to cause instantaneous death, with such determined purpose did they appear to have been inflicted. The instrument

Newspaper account of the trial of highway-robber William Thompson.

ANOTHER UNSUCCESSFUL HIGHWAYMAN

Not all highwaymen were accomplished in their law-breaking or successful in their exploits. Another local example was a character called Walker, an opportunistic highwayman, who was drawn into a life of crime in order to fund his other nefarious activities. On Sunday, 12 January 1777, he attempted to rob the Norwich stagecoach, 1½ miles outside of Newmarket in Suffolk. He was armed only with an iron candlestick, but did manage to stop the coach. Unfortunately for him, one of the passengers took exception to the highwayman's approach and shot at him. Walker dug his spurs into his horse and attempted to make off, but rode only a few yards before falling to the ground. He was picked up and carried to the Red Lion Inn in Newmarket, where he died an hour later. It transpired that the 23 year old had inherited a considerable fortune some years before and had led a depraved life in London before taking up his later illicit profession. He died leaving a wife and children in the city.

Later that evening, Thompson had apparently bought some pork chops from a butcher's, paying for them with an old bill for 5 shillings, which he pulled from an unusual canvas purse. While there, a woman had entered the shop to announce that the dead body of Lorenz Beha had been found and the butcher observed that on hearing the news, Thompson began to 'tremble like an aspen leaf'. The witnesses had also noted that the young man had been dressed in a suit that was much cleaner than that which Thompson usually wore.

The jury took only a few minutes to return a verdict of 'Guilty'. In passing the sentence of death upon the prisoner, the trial judge announced that his guilt had been proved by the clearest and most conclusive evidence he had ever seen. The *Ipswich Journal* reported later that Thompson had listened to the judge's address without any display of emotion 'as though he had merely been sentenced to a day's imprisonment for a petty larceny'.

THE EXECUTION

In the days following the trial, it emerged that Thompson had a clear motive to kill Beha. He had apparently purchased a watch for £6 and 5 shillings from the jeweller on one of Beha's earlier rounds and had agreed to pay for the item in instalments. Knowing that Beha would be calling on him for a further payment, Thompson recognised that he had insufficient funds for the next instalment and had devised a different form of payback.

William Thompson was hanged on Castle Hill in Norwich on Saturday, 8 April 1854. By all accounts it was not a quick execution, one newspaper later reporting that 'the criminal's struggles continued for five minutes'.

The body of Lorenz Beha was eventually laid to rest in a tomb within the Roman Catholic church on London Road in King's Lynn – the victim of a brutal and premeditated highway robbery.

1855

MRS FISHER ESCAPES THE NOOSE

IN THE ANNALS of crime, the nineteenth century has often been portrayed as the poisoner's heyday – a time when deadly chemicals and concoctions were readily obtained, easily administered and frequently difficult to detect in charges of murder. Norwich and the county of Norfolk more generally had a spate of poisoning cases throughout the period. They were symptomatic of what many felt was a growing social problem.

A FASHIONABLE CRIME

An illustration of this comes from the 1852 trial of William Rollinson, an 80-year-old Suffolk man found guilty of murdering Ann Cornell by arsenic poisoning. In his summing up, the trial judge, Lord Chief Justice Campbell, reflected that: 'This crime of poisoning has reached a frequency in this and the adjoining county [by which he meant Norfolk] that is altogether appalling ... A terrible example must be made to deter others from following so wicked a course.'

Four years later, Lord Campbell would preside over the trial of arguably the most famous of the nineteenth-century poisoners, namely, Dr William Palmer – the 'Rugeley Poisoner' – who despatched his victims using antimony in order to claim on the insurance policies he had taken out on them. His conviction would in fact lead to a new Act of Parliament, commonly referred to as 'Palmer's Act' which made it unlawful to take out an insurance policy on someone else's life.

However, a year before this, the trial judge oversaw a case brought against a Norwich woman accused of poisoning her husband with prussic acid. In his opening address to the Grand Jury at the Norfolk Lent Assizes in March 1855,

Lord Chief Justice Campbell – the judge in the trial of Mary Anne Fisher. He presided over many other sensational cases of murder by poison.

Lord Campbell indicated that of the fourteen trials facing them, that of Mary Anne Fisher was the 'most serious case' and indicated that 'The circumstances were somewhat remarkable.' And indeed they were, although in this particular Norfolk poisoning case, the outcome of the trial was to be very different to that anticipated by the public and press.

'OH, WHAT A JOB! GEORGE IS DEAD!'

On Wednesday, 29 November 1854, George Fisher had expected to go to work in his job as a wood turner. He had talked to people about it, having recently been restored to health after suffering a rupture and succumbing to a severe bout of constipation the previous month, for which he had been treated by local surgeon Mr Morgan. As it transpired, he never saw the light of day that Wednesday. For the evening before, his wife, Mary Anne Fisher, had roused his brother William – who lived nearby – to say that George was dying, before hurrying on to wake up her uncle.

On arriving at the house, William found his brother stretched out on his back, with his eyes staring wide and his jaw moving up and down, writhing as if he was trying to throw something off his stomach. Unbeknown to his sibling, George was in the last throes of death, having been poisoned by hydrogen cyanide – a colourless, extremely toxic liquid otherwise known as prussic acid. Mr Morgan was called and was shocked to find that the patient he had earlier passed off as fit to return to work was now, unexpectedly and rather bizarrely,

fading fast. Within minutes, George Fisher had passed away and shortly afterwards his wife arrived back at the house with some of her neighbours to 'lay out' the corpse.

On the following day, Mrs Fisher and the family applied to Mr Morgan for the required burial certificate, but the astute doctor refused to provide one, saying that the death was unaccountable to him and proposing that a post-mortem examination be carried out. At first, the family protested, but eventually Morgan was allowed to take the corpse away for analysis. On opening the body, the doctor was aware of a powerful and peculiar odour – an almond-like essence – which satisfied him immediately that the cause of death was poisoning by prussic acid. He went on to find traces of it in the deceased's stomach.

When the doctor's conclusions were broadcast to the family, Mary Fisher exclaimed: 'Good God! Why I got it for him myself,' and went on to say that at George's request she had purchased the previous evening 'two-pennyworth of something' which she could not at first recollect the name of, but, on reflection, remembered that it was 'essential oil of almonds'. Her husband had written the name of the substance down on a piece of paper, which she had subsequently returned to him with the poison. In the investigations that followed, no trace was ever found of either the note or the bottle in which the acid had been dispensed.

SUSPICIONS ARE AROUSED

The suspicions surrounding Mary Fisher continued to grow when enquiries in the neighbourhood revealed that she had been endeavouring to purchase a quantity of arsenic for about three weeks. Her conversations with colleagues at the factory of Messrs J. Sultzer & Company where she worked had been concerned with the best method for 'stilling' her mother and she had asked a number of people what two local tradesmen had taken to poison themselves in recent suicide cases. The answer, she learnt, from a colleague called Spencer, was 'essential oil of almonds'. In responding to this, she said: 'It would have been a good job, then, if my old mother had taken some years ago.'

It was further revealed that, on the Saturday before George Fisher's demise, his wife had tried (without success) to obtain a quantity of prussic acid from Mr Watson, a chemist on King Street, some distance from her home. She claimed to live on St Faith's Lane in Norwich and said that the acid was needed by her husband who was a dyer and used it in his trade. The druggist refused to dispense the poison. Two days later, she successfully obtained two-pennyworth of prussic acid from another chemist, J.H. Hulme, on St Andrews Hall Plain, explaining that while she knew he should not ordinarily dispense it, he could be reassured that her husband ('a worker in chemicals') had bought it before and had been given written authority to purchase it by Mr Morgan the doctor – something which the surgeon would later deny emphatically. In making the purchase, she obtained two phials: one labelled 'Poison', the other marked 'Essential Oil of Almonds'.

THE CORONER'S INQUEST

As a result of Mr Morgan's post-mortem, a coroner's jury was convened to examine the circumstances surrounding the death. This was chaired by William Wilde, coroner for the city of Norwich. As well as hearing the conclusions from Mr Morgan's post-mortem examination and testimony about Mary Fisher's earlier discussions about the properties of various poisons, the coroner's jury also learned that her mother had recently borrowed a sum of money from a loan society and that George Fisher and his brother-in-law had provided sureties on the loan. When the old lady had been unable to repay the borrowed amount, Fisher had been asked to pay regular instalments of 10 shillings – something which he had found difficult being ill and out of work.

Mr Spencer, who worked with Mary at the Sultzer factory, told the jury that she had knocked on his door on the morning of the death, exclaiming: 'Oh, what a job! George is dead! I shall never get over it. He has taken poison.' She recounted her earlier conversation with him about the properties of prussic acid and he had asked her why she had obtained some when he had indicated clearly that it was a 'rank poison'. Mary apparently said that George had been in the habit of purchasing different chemicals to stain wood and he had asked her to buy the prussic acid for that purpose. She had added that she did not believe it to be a poison as she knew of someone who had taken it as a remedy for a particular ailment. Having complied with her husband's request, she had left the bottle on the mantelpiece and had

OTHER NOTABLE CASES OF POISONING IN NINETEENTH-CENTURY NORFOLK

1825 – The Neal family – mother Mary, and her children Susan and William – were tried for the attempted murder of William Hales, his family and a servant girl, using white arsenic. Found guilty, they were due to be hanged, but had their sentences commuted to transportation to Australia for life.

1829 – John Stratford was found guilty of the murder of John Burgess and hanged in Norwich at the city gaol on Monday, 17 August. His chosen poison was arsenic.

1833 – Mary Wright was found guilty of poisoning her husband with arsenic. It had been mixed into a plum cake. She died in Norwich Castle on 1 November before she could be transported.

1835/36 – The sensational 'Burnham Poisoners' were tried and executed for murder. Frances Billing had despatched Mary Taylor, while Catherine Frarey had killed her own husband. Both had used arsenic to poison their victims.

Left *Death mask of the 'Burnham Poisoner' Frances Billing.*

Right *Death mask of the 'Burnham Poisoner' Catherine Frary.*

gone out that Tuesday evening to visit a Mrs Clarke, who had been very kind to her and her husband.

The jury heard testimony from neighbours that Mary had lived comfortably with her husband and had been attentive to him during his periods of illness. They also learned that George had been depressed as a result of his illness and the financial pressures of having to meet the loan repayments. The suggestion was that the deceased had taken his own life by drinking the prussic acid while Mary was absent from the house that Tuesday evening. The flaw here was a significant and tangible one – no trace had been found of the poison bottle apparently left on the mantelpiece and it was unlikely that the deceased could have disposed of it himself.

The coroner's jury clearly had their concerns about the nature of the death. At the conclusion of the inquiry, Mary was committed to take her trial on a charge of poisoning her husband with essential oil of almonds. She was taken back into custody, having been housed in Norwich Gaol since the start of the proceedings. The *Bury and Norwich Post* reported her response to the outcome: 'The prisoner, who has obstinately refused food for three days, received the verdict with listless indifference and not a word escaped her lips.'

THE COUNTY COURT TRIAL

In the days following the coroner's verdict, the local and national press appeared to be in no doubt that the poisoning was an open and shut case. One newspaper reported that: 'The deceased, who was recovering from a protracted indisposition, is supposed to have been killed by his wife that she might avoid payment of a weekly instalment of 2s 6d due on a loan! At least, no other motive is apparent.'

On Thursday, 11 January 1855, a hearing by Norwich magistrates completed the pre-trial formalities, with Mary being committed for trial at the forthcoming Lent Assizes.

The county trial began on Saturday, 24 March. All of the testimony presented at the coroner's inquest was replayed for the benefit of the court. They heard how Mary Fisher had at various times made statements to people suggesting that she wished to get rid of her husband. One witness reported her saying that, 'He was better, and she had thought to have croaked him this time, but he had licked her now,' and to another, 'He was better, but she was disappointed, as she hoped to have come to work in a new black dress very soon.' It was also established that the quantity of prussic acid which the accused had purchased – some 40 drops – was more than sufficient to cause death.

New testimony included a statement from the wife of a constable who had spoken to Mary after the coroner's inquest. She claimed that the accused had told her that on the evening of 28 November, she had gone out to see a friend and had returned at half-past ten to find her husband in bed. Mary had also ventured that Mr Morgan had changed her husband's medicine – something which the doctor was again to refute under oath.

Following the case for the prosecution, Mr Dasent did a remarkable job of defending his client. He submitted that there was no evidence for any motive in the case. In fact, the case against Mrs Fisher 'depended on the recollection of loose and vague expressions'. He also pointed to the testimony of the individuals who had suggested that the Fishers 'lived happily together' and that Mary had provided her husband with all of the care and attention that might be expected during his period of illness. He put it to the jury that the more charitable and rational explanation for what had occurred was that George Fisher had administered the poison himself, either by accident or design, during his wife's absence. He stressed that the deceased was, at the time of death, 'ill in body, out of work, and depressed in spirits, in consequence of his liability for his mother-in-law'.

The jury retired to consider their verdict and after an absence of only half an hour, returned to announce that they believed the prisoner to be 'Not Guilty'. There were gasps of surprise in the courtroom. Mary Anne Fisher had been acquitted in a most remarkable trial.

THE AFTERMATH

It was clear from the press reports after the trial that the newspapers had firmly believed Mary Fisher to be guilty of murder. One – announcing the acquittal – went on to say: 'The deceased died from the effects of prussic acid and it was proved that the prisoner had, a short time previously, purchased a quantity of essential oil of almonds sufficient to cause his death. She had also, at various times, let fall various expressions indicating a desire to get rid of her husband.' It was hardly an endorsement of the decision to acquit the accused.

The trial was one of many East Anglian cases which highlighted the popular obsession with poisoning. In the nineteenth century it had become a favourite topic with the press, described by some commentators as a 'fashionable' Victorian crime which was out of control. As poisoning could be done in secrecy and its detection relied mainly on circumstantial evidence and the rudimentary – albeit rapidly developing – science of toxicology, it is little wonder that it was perceived to be an easy form of murder.

In reality, there was no poisoning epidemic and the number of reported cases of criminal poisoning remained fairly constant throughout the century. Most cases served only to demonstrate how the criminal justice system was getting more adept at investigating and prosecuting those who were tempted to misuse the contents of the poison cabinet. Most, that is, except in the case of Mary Anne Smith, who might be said to have escaped the noose with more than a pinch of good luck.

LETHAL IN SMALL DOSES – THE CHOICE OF POISONERS THROUGHOUT THE AGES

Mercury – most deaths involving this element have been accidental, e.g. the Minamata Bay disaster of the 1950s, where mercury was discharged into the sea in Japan and poisoned the fish eaten by locals. Murderers that have used it include Mary Bateman, who was hanged on 20 March 1809, for poisoning Rebecca Perrigo.

Arsenic – the most common poison used in murder. Although the natural arsenic minerals orpiment and realgar are poisonous, the most reliable state in which to administer arsenic is in its oxide form.

Antimony – gram for gram, antimony is almost as toxic as arsenic, but is usually less effective as antimony salts rapidly cause vomiting, expelling the toxins before they can be absorbed.

Lead – numerous small doses of this element can be assimilated by the body with deadly effects. The body's response to a sudden large dose is usually to expel it through sickness or diarrhoea.

Thallium – thallium sulphate is soluble in water, colourless and virtually tasteless. A fatal amount can also be given in a single dose.

1874

THE GREAT RAILWAY DISASTER

THE BIRTH OF the steam locomotive and the development of the railway network brought widespread and wholesale changes to all aspects of social and economic life in Victorian Britain. With reduced travelling times and significantly lower transport costs, the railways became the lifeblood of the Industrial Revolution and contributed much to the growing prosperity of the nation. As elsewhere, East Anglia enjoyed its own period of 'railway mania' in the 1840s – the Eastern Union Railway completing the route from London to Norwich via Ipswich in 1849, and a number of smaller companies building individual lines to connect with the main arterial routes. In August 1862, all of these companies were incorporated into the new Great Eastern Railway (GER).

While being a positive force for change in so many ways, the operation of the railway network was not without its challenges and pitfalls. First and foremost was the need to standardise time and operating schedules, which most railway companies began to address in the 1840s. This had become an absolute necessity, with trains running at ever-increasing speeds and locomotive drivers needing to negotiate the rapidly expanding number of railway junctions. Unsurprisingly, the frequency of rail accidents was high, and it was only in the latter part of the nineteenth century that comprehensive signalling and 'block telegraph' systems began to be introduced to prevent collisions between different trains operating on single-track lines.

The necessity for these innovations was demonstrated most clearly and tragically by a rail disaster at Thorpe, near Norwich, on the night of Thursday, 10 September 1874. It remains one of the worst head-on collisions in British railway history.

The scene of the railway disaster at Thorpe.

78

A DISASTER WAITING TO HAPPEN

At the time of the accident, the Great Eastern route from Norwich to Great Yarmouth included a 6-mile section of single track which ran from Thorpe Junction – about a quarter of a mile from the Norwich Thorpe station – towards Brundall. It seems likely that the company had already recognised the risks of operating the single-track line which carried both local traffic and the faster express trains which ran to and from Great Yarmouth. Elsewhere, it had already begun the process of introducing double lines of rails to replace single-track workings.

At half-past nine on the evening of the disaster, a mail train travelling towards Norwich met a fast-moving express train heading in the opposite direction. For reasons which would become clearer in the weeks to follow, the accident had resulted from human error. However, the conditions at the point of impact had not helped. The rails were slippery from heavy rainfall and there was a slight curve in the line at the fatal spot, so that the lights of neither train could be seen and both drivers had little time to apply their brakes.

A FRIGHTFUL ACCIDENT

The engine drawing the mail train (No. 54) was the more modern, powerful and heavier of the two locomotives. While lighter, the express train had gathered considerable momentum and it was estimated later that the engines had met head-on at a combined speed of around 50mph. Little wonder, then, that the final death toll from the accident reached twenty-five, with a further

The wreck of the trains after the collision.

ANOTHER HEAD-ON COLLISION

—⊶⊷—

Norwich Thorpe station was to witness another head-on collision between two steam locomotives on the early morning of Thursday, 3 February 1949. At 6.33 a.m., as the Norwich to Ely passenger train was leaving its platform, it was routed accidentally onto a line being used by an incoming Whitemoor to Norwich freight train. On this occasion there were no fatalities, although the drivers of both engines, as well as the fireman and guard of the freight train, sustained minor injuries. The front ends of both engines were heavily damaged and some wheels had been derailed. A subsequent inquiry for the Ministry of Transport concluded that a mistake by a signalman had been the primary cause of the collision.

—⊶⊷—

seventy-three passengers and staff being seriously injured.

With the impact of the crash, the funnel of engine No. 54 was wrenched away from the locomotive as the express train meeting it was launched high up into the air. Carriages from both trains followed, until a pyramid of debris – some 60–70ft high – was formed from the tangled engines, shattered carriages and dead, dying and wounded passengers. The loud hissing of steam contributed to the overwhelming cacophony of sound.

First to meet their deaths had been the drivers and firemen from both trains, who were killed instantly. The crash was heard throughout the village of Thorpe, and many locals rushed to the scene of the disaster to offer what assistance they could to the dying and wounded. Within a short space of time, a relief train had been despatched from Norwich Thorpe station, carrying railway workers and a number of doctors and medical staff.

THE TERRIBLE AFTERMATH

Working from the light of the still-burning carriages, the railway officials and medical men began to clear away the debris and recover the dead and wounded passengers. The injured were then transported to the Norfolk and Norwich Hospital, while the bodies of those found dead were laid out in a nearby boathouse and a room at the Three Tuns tavern in Thorpe.

While many survivors emerged from the crash scene with burns, the heavy rain which had continued to fall throughout the evening did help to dampen the numerous small fires which might otherwise have consumed the pyramid of debris. And while the scale of the human disaster was grim enough, other factors had helped to mitigate the loss of life. The train from Norwich had just passed over a wooden bridge crossing the River Yare; had the collision occurred on the bridge itself, it is likely that many of the passengers surviving the immediate impact would have drowned in the icy cold water. Similarly, while the mail train was crowded with

passengers who had earlier attended a flower show in Lowestoft, they were positioned towards the rear of the train and most emerged from the crash comparatively unscathed.

The recovery operation continued into the night, although it was only on the afternoon of the following day that the track was finally cleared and normal rail traffic resumed.

THE CRASH INVESTIGATION

On Saturday, 12 September, the President of the Board of Trade asked for a formal inquiry into the circumstances surrounding the collision. The report, which was delivered to Parliament at the end of the month, criticised the laxity of the GER procedures that had allowed the disaster to occur and concluded that: 'This is the most serious collision between trains meeting one another on a single line of rails, if not the most serious rail catastrophe as regards the number of lives lost and serious injuries, that has yet been experienced in this country.'

The enquiry uncovered a series of errors and misunderstandings between the stationmaster, a night inspector and

The immediate aftermath of the Norwich railway collision in 1874.

a telegraph clerk, which had contributed to the calamity. This had resulted in the despatch of a message without a required signature which had, in turn, allowed both trains to enter onto the single-track line with fatal results. The report highlighted some of the changes which could be introduced to improve rail safety, including the use of the block-telegraph system to improve rail communications.

DEATH BY FIRING SQUAD

EDITH CAVELL IS rightly regarded as one of the most inspiring and heroic figures of the First World War. Yet her devotion to duty and bravery in the face of enemy hostility was driven as much by her strong Anglican faith and moral fortitude as it was by her belief in the righteousness of the conflict with Germany. Steadfast in her selflessness and obdurate to any of the threats that she faced, the Norfolk-born nurse has been martyred since her death as a true British heroine. So how was it that this pioneering health worker met her fate at the hands of the German military in the full glare of the international press?

HUMBLE BEGINNINGS

Edith Louisa Cavell was born on 4 December 1865 in the small village of Swardeston, some 4 miles south of Norwich. Her father was the Reverend Frederick Cavell, who had been the local vicar for less than two years and served a community of less than 400.

As the eldest of four children, Edith was raised as a Conformist and educated

to believe in the importance of fundamental Christian principles: salvation through prayer, sharing with the less fortunate and devotion to others before oneself. It was these values that came to define her professional career long before the shadow of war was to creep across Europe.

By all accounts, Edith enjoyed her childhood – later describing the period

Portrait of Edith Cavell. (Library of Congress, LC-DIG-ggbain-20268)

when 'life was fresh and beautiful and the country so desirable and sweet'. Encouraged by her father to lead by example, the youngster took up many charitable activities, including the production of some drawings for greetings cards in 1885 to raise money for the local Sunday school. Alongside her father's stern approach to religious devotion, Edith also appears to have adopted her mother Louisa's more tender ways, focusing more on the practical application of Christian values rather than the strict doctrinal theories of her faith. It was an approach that was to serve her well in later life.

EDITH THE GOVERNESS

From the age of 17, Edith spent time in three different girls' boarding schools. Her private education was designed to prepare her for a traditional middle-class marriage or – if she were to remain unmarried – to equip her to gain useful employment as a governess with a respectable family. There was little attention given to those subjects or academic pursuits which may have led an independent woman to pursue any form of professional career. Nevertheless, this education did enable Edith to develop an aptitude for languages and created within her a desire to travel and see more of the world.

At 5ft 3in, with dark wavy hair, the pretty 21 year old returned home to her family in the summer of 1886. Through her father's connections, she then embarked on a career as a governess, first with the family of an Essex vicar and later with a family in Brussels. Spending five years with the wealthy and bourgeois François family, she became the governess to three girls and a boy between the ages of 13 and 3. While the position provided her with a chance to travel and a social standing in Belgian society that belied her humble origins, the job did little to bring her into contact with anyone of her own age or nationality and provided even less opportunity to meet any potential partners. In 1895, she left the job, returning home to nurse her sick father, an early demonstration of the caring and devotion to service which would become the focus of her life in later years.

THE ENGLISH NURSE

Like her two sisters, Edith was to take up nursing as a profession. At 30 years of age, she began work as an assistant nurse at the Fountains Fever Hospital in Tooting, London. Helping to treat patients with fevers ranging from typhus, cholera and smallpox to diphtheria, influenza, tuberculosis and measles, she threw herself into the demanding role with characteristic vigour. The hours were long, many of the tasks menial, and the rules for ward staff strict and regimented. Above all, it was the care of the patients that came first.

In the seven months that she spent at the 'Fountains', Edith decided that she wanted to pursue more formal training in the profession and applied to become a probationer nurse at the London Hospital. In September 1896, she formally entered the profession that was to define her life and ultimately map out her destiny. From the start it proved to be a difficult path to tread.

In her training as a probationer, Edith gathered knowledge and experience in all facets of nursing and within two years passed the examinations for her London Hospital certificate, which qualified her as a staff nurse. Despite this, the Matron of London Hospital delivered a less than flattering evaluation of her performance: 'Edith Cavell had plenty of capability for her work when she chose to exert herself, but she was not very much in earnest, not at all punctual and not a Nurse that could altogether be depended upon ...'

In the months that followed, Edith operated outside of the hospital tending to the needs of specific patients: an Ilford man with terminal cancer, a 14-year-old boy with typhoid in West Norwood and an 80 year old with gout in Gloucester.

She continued to work long and hard in all of the various roles she took on for the next eight years and in late 1906 accepted a temporary post as Matron of a private nursing institution in Manchester. The increased responsibility included managing the nursing staff and dealing with the budget and all of the administration for the home. Although the appointment was temporary, it provided Edith with invaluable experience for her final and most substantive posting.

A MATRON IN BRUSSELS

In May 1907, Edith Cavell accepted an offer to become Matron of the first nurse training school to be established in Brussels, under leading surgeon Dr Antoine Depage. With her significant nursing expertise, fluent French and previous experience of working in Belgium, she was felt to be the ideal candidate.

In the years to come, Edith was instrumental in establishing the school as one of the finest nursing schools in Belgium and a model of good practice for nurse training. It also became her home and she surrounded herself with the few familiar items she possessed and took in a stray dog, which she named Jack. He was to become a much-loved companion.

Back in Norfolk, Edith's father retired in 1909 and was obliged to move out of the vicarage in Swardeston. He and Louisa moved to No. 24 College Road, a terraced house in Norwich. In June of the following year, the Reverend Cavell died and Edith returned home for the funeral. Thereafter she tried to encourage her mother to move to Brussels and live with her at the nursing school but, after a short sojourn in December 1910, Louisa returned home to Norwich, where she would spend the rest of her life. Edith would then travel back to Norwich each summer to be with her family and to celebrate her mother's birthday on 6 July.

WAR IS DECLARED

In the summer of 1914, during one of Edith's long-awaited Norfolk holidays, the news was dominated by the murder in Bosnia of Archduke Franz-Ferdinand, heir to the Austro-Hungarian throne. His death, at the hands of a Serb nationalist on 28 June, was the catalyst which would lead inexorably to the outbreak of hostilities in Europe and the First World War.

While Edith enjoyed the long hot summer with her family and friends, the European powers were declaring their positions and aligning themselves with the two sides of the conflict. The Austro-Hungarian Empire declared war on Serbia on 28 July. Two days later, Russia mobilised its 6 million troops and prepared to invade Austria. In response, both Austria and Germany mobilised their forces and declared martial law.

As the tense stand-off continued, Edith received a telegram from the nursing school in Brussels expressing fears about the escalation of the conflict. Switzerland, Holland and Belgium had mobilised their small armies and all communications between Belgium and Germany were effectively suspended.

The following day – Sunday, 2 August – Germany declared war on Russia, marched into Luxembourg and issued an ultimatum to the Belgian government to allow German troops to march through the country in preparation for an attack on France. The communiqué stated that any refusal to allow this would be considered an act of hostility.

While the mayhem ensued, Edith Cavell made preparations to return to Belgium, recognising that her nursing skills would be needed to treat the inevitable casualties of any conflict. She eventually reached Brussels in the early hours of the next morning. That same day, King Albert of Belgium informed the Kaiser that German troops could not advance onto neutral Belgian soil and any attempt to do so would be resisted with all possible means.

On 4 August, the Kaiser ignored the King's protestations and gave orders for the invasion of Belgium, pushing Britain to declare war on Germany. Edith now found herself in charge of a Belgian nursing school in the undefended city of Brussels, which was about to be overrun by an enemy power. The prospects did not look good.

NURSING IN WARTIME

As Britain prepared to send an Expeditionary Force to push German troops out of Belgium, Edith Cavell wrote a feature for the *Nursing Mirror* in which she stated: 'We were full of enthusiasm for the war and full of confidence in the Allies.' Her faith was to be short-lived. On the afternoon of 20 August, thousands of German troops began to march through Brussels en route to Paris. Edith would write later, 'The sun shone in mockery on our fallen hopes ...'

For the nurses at the Belgian School of Nursing, the occupation signalled no cessation of their daily duties. Edith sought to reassure her terrified staff and made it clear that any injured soldiers brought in must be attended to – whatever their nationality. Even in a time of war, she believed that her caring professional duties outweighed any nationalistic concerns. Throughout the period of conflict, the school would continue to operate along these lines.

RESISTING THE GERMANS

The Germans were quick to exert their military authority over the city. A Governor General was appointed and a network of soldiers, sentries and spies were used to enforce the occupation and control all aspects of daily life. This included a night-time curfew, restrictions on travel, control over the postal service and house-to-house searches.

As the deprivations continued, Edith became one of only a handful of English citizens left in Brussels. Doctor Depage offered to arrange for her to be smuggled out of the city, but she resisted, wanting only to play her part in nursing the sick.

Resistance to the Germans began to develop into a familiar pattern of activities in support of the growing number of Allied soldiers that managed to escape the clutches of the German military as fighting on the Western Front intensified – passing messages, providing maps and shelter, sharing food, and helping with clothing, identity papers and disguises. Over time, an informal network of citizens began to play an active part in assisting these soldiers to escape and cross into Holland. It was a risky business, viewed by the Germans as a hostile act, and subject to harsh punishments. From November 1914, Edith Cavell became a key player within all of this, helping to provide shelter and passage for these 'lost children' and working with others to furnish an escape route for over 200 servicemen through to the summer of the following year.

ASSISTING THE FUGITIVES

Fugitive British, French and Belgian soldiers were sheltered, fed and hidden from the German authorities by Prince Reginald de Croÿ at a château near Mons. The location became a key part of the wider resistance movement.

From here, the escapees were provided with false papers and taken by guides to various safe houses, including that of Edith Cavell. From these locations, the displaced soldiers were provided with money and assistance to reach the Dutch frontier.

Back home at College Road in Norwich, Louisa Cavell began to receive correspondence from many of the British troops who managed to successfully reach England. They told of Edith's kindness and courage in helping them to escape and reported that she was well. It was little comfort to the ageing widow, who grew increasingly fearful about the dangers of her daughter's activities.

Over the coming months, the German authorities began to impose tougher restrictions on the movement of Belgian citizens and harsher penalties on those found guilty of assisting fugitive soldiers in an effort to break the resistance. Their network of spies also began to hear rumours of the involvement of an English nurse in the escape network. It was only a matter of time before Edith Cavell would come under the spotlight and, in the period until the end of July 1915, she found herself under the surveillance of the secret police.

On 3 August, Edith was finally arrested and charged with harbouring Allied soldiers in contravention of German military law. It appeared that she had been betrayed by George Gaston Quien, an agent provocateur and German collaborator. As part of his subterfuge, he had arrived at the nursing school in June, posing as a wounded French soldier and asking for Cavell's assistance in escaping to Holland.

Edith was held in the main Brussels prison of St Gilles for the next ten weeks, the final two weeks of her incarceration spent in solitary confinement. Throughout August she made three statements in French under interrogation, admitting her involvement in sheltering and assisting derelict Allied soldiers. The depositions she signed were written in German – she had no way of knowing whether they accurately reflected what she had said.

THE COURT MARTIAL

At the military trial in October 1915, Edith was prosecuted for her admission of guilt in aiding combatants to cross the Dutch border and make their way to Britain. Her assertion that many of the soldiers she had helped to escape had thanked her in writing when arriving back in Britain only added to the prosecution's contrived case against her. Found guilty under the German Military Code, Edith was sentenced to death for her treason in 'Conducting soldiers to the enemy'.

The British government and a plethora of foreign diplomats and dignitaries made last-ditch efforts to secure a commutation of her sentence in the days that followed. But it was all too little, too late. In the late afternoon of Monday, 11 October, she was informed by the German prison chaplain that the death penalty against her would be carried out at seven o'clock the following morning.

SHOT AT DAWN

That night, before her final night's sleep, Edith was seen by the Reverend Stirling Gahan, an Anglican chaplain who had been given permission to visit her. She was resolute against the ordeal she was about to face, saying:

> I have no fear or shrinking. I have seen death so often it is not strange or fearful to me. Life has always been hurried and full of difficulty. This time of rest has been a great mercy. Everyone here has been very kind.
>
> But I would say, standing as I do in view of God and Eternity: I realise that patriotism is not enough. I must have no hatred or bitterness towards anyone.

The following morning, the English Matron was driven by car from the prison to a German shooting range on the outskirts of Brussels, along with others found guilty of treason. They were walked to some vertical stakes in front of a muddy slope to face two rows of eight armed soldiers. Bound to the execution post with a bandage across her eyes, Edith awaited the signal to fire. When it was given, the shots rang out. One bullet went through her forehead, another through her heart.

THE AFTERMATH

Immediately after the execution, Edith's body was buried in an unmarked cemetery close to the firing range. Her execution at the hands of the German military sparked a media sensation and established her as an iconic propaganda figure for military recruitment. 'Let Cavell be the battle cry', announced the *Daily Graphic* in a campaign to bolster continuing public support for the war in the trenches. The publicity surrounding her death doubled the recruitment of volunteers in Britain from 5,000 to 10,000 each week in the two months that followed. It also helped to convince a sceptical public that military conscription was required – a campaign that began in January 1916.

The British and US press revelled in the 'moral depravity' and 'barbarism' of the Prussian military machine. The German government continued to assert its view that it had acted fairly and in accordance with military law.

THE LASTING MEMORY

Despite the wishes of the Cavell family that Edith's passing be marked with 'no monuments', the country erected more commemorative plaques and statues to her than any other woman of the period. This was later to include the iconic 10ft-high marble statue that sits on top of a granite column at St Martin's Place in London, close to Nelson's Column in Trafalgar Square.

On 12 October 1918 – the third anniversary of her death – Norwich paid its own tribute to the departed Norfolk nurse with the unveiling of a carved memorial in Tombland. The sculpture by Henry Alfred Pegram consists of a bronze bust of Edith on a stone pillar, beneath which a soldier holds up a laurel wreath. The inscription reads: 'Edith Cavell, Nurse, Patriot and Martyr.' In 1983, this monument was moved

Postcard photograph of Edith Cavell's original grave site in Belgium.

to where it now sits alongside the Erpingham Gate of the cathedral.

After the war, Edith's remains were exhumed from her unmarked Belgian grave and returned to Britain for a state funeral at Westminster Abbey. But it was in Norwich that she was to be finally laid to rest. On 19 May 1919, she was reburied in a simple grave at the eastern side of Norwich Cathedral in an area known as Life's Green.

History has portrayed Edith Cavell in the various stereotypes of 'innocent victim', 'devoted patriot' and 'faithful Christian'. All have some grounding in fact, and after the passage of almost 100 years since her fateful firing squad, she is still held in esteem as a national heroine, her stoicism forever intact – a genuine Norfolk martyr.

EDITH CAVELL – LONG-REMEMBERED NURSE

Since the First World War, Edith Cavell has been venerated at home and abroad for her resistance to the German military authorities in Belgium. Memorials have included not just those in London and Norwich. There is a stone statue by Canadian sculptor R. Tait McKenzie in the garden behind the Red Cross National (US) Headquarters in Washington DC and a marble and stone memorial near The Shrine in Melbourne, Australia.

Medical and nursing facilities have been named in her honour, including the Edith Cavell Hospital in the Brussels borough of Uccle and the Edith Cavell Regional School of Nursing in Belleville, Ontario, Canada. The UK, Canada, Australia, India and Argentina also have schools named after her, not least of which is the Cavell Primary and Nursery School in Norwich.

Street names also abound, including 'Cavell Road' in Norwich, Billericay and Dudley, and 'Cavell Street' in Whitechapel (London), West Hobart (Tasmania), Dunedin (New Zealand) and Reefton (New Zealand). And there are also parks, playgrounds, bridges and geographical features bearing Cavell's name in various parts of the world.

In popular culture, the 1939 US film *Nurse Edith Cavell*, directed by Herbert Wilcox, portrayed the ill-fated Matron with Anna Neagle in the title role. French singer and international diva Édith Piaf – born Édith Giovanna Gassion in Belleville, Paris, on 15 December 1915 – was also named after the Norfolk nurse.

Edith Cavell memorial in Tombland.

Life's Green in Norwich Cathedral – final resting place of Edith Cavell.

1942

THE BAEDEKER BLITZ

ON **28 MARCH** 1942, over 200 British bombers took off for a massive air raid on Germany. Their target was the Baltic port of Lübeck in Northern Germany, the second largest city in the Schleswig-Holstein state, the ancient heart of which was composed mainly of wooden buildings. The bombs and incendiaries dropped that night devastated the city and left over 1,000 civilians dead. It would trigger a significant reprisal by the Germans against Britain and put Norwich in the firing line as part of what became known as the 'Baedeker Raids'.

HITLER SEES RED

Adolf Hitler was enraged by the British bombing of Lübeck and gave orders for a new bombing campaign against historical towns and cities across England. The Luftwaffe selected a number of militarily insignificant but picturesque locations and conducted raids in two tranches between April and June 1942. The targets were said to have been chosen from Baedeker's Great

Britain tourist guide as having historical significance.

The first raid occurred on the night of 23 April, when Exeter was attacked by twenty-five Luftwaffe bombers, leaving seventy dead and considerable destruction across the city. The following day, Baron Gustav Braun von Sturm – a Nazi propagandist – was quoted as saying: 'We shall go out and bomb every building in Britain marked with three stars in the Baedeker Guide.'

Exeter was attacked that same night and a few days later there were similar raids on Bath, York and Norwich – the latter occurring on 27 and 29 April.

NORWICH PREPARES FOR ATTACK

Like other major conurbations, Norwich had taken steps in the early part of the Second World War to prepare for an air attack by the Germans. Public air-raid shelters were constructed and important buildings were shored up and protected by sandbags. Volunteer Air Raid Precautions (ARP) Wardens were also enlisted to assist with civil

Air-raid sandbags at the Guildhall in 1939. (George Plunkett)

defence and some citizens built their own Anderson or Morrison shelters to protect against the bombs. The first air-raid siren sounded on the very day that war was declared, although it was not until 9 July 1940 that the first attack on the city would be felt.

It was widely recognised prior to the war that Norwich was vulnerable to air attack. The city itself, many nearby towns and a number of military installations that were dotted around Norfolk, made the area a significant target for German bombers, which also criss-crossed the county en route to other destinations and occasionally jettisoned their bombs before returning home across the North Sea.

As the conflict unfolded, Norwich and its rural hinterland were provided with a network of anti-aircraft and searchlight batteries, barrage balloons and anti-landing trenches to counter the threat of aerial attack. In September 1941, the first secret radar system was also installed at the new radar station

of RAF Neatishead to the north-east of Norwich. This provided a Ground Control Intercept station, which could direct Royal Air Force fighters – both day and night – to attack any enemy aircraft that launched attacks on Norwich and other targets in Norfolk.

THE BOMBS BEGIN TO FALL

Throughout 1940 there were sporadic air raids on Norwich, with most damage and loss of life occurring mainly in the residential areas of the city. Of the sixty people killed in raids that year, twenty-six died during the first raid on 9 July. A key industrial target that was hit a number of times was the Boulton and Paul Riverside Engineering Works, which sustained a major fire on 1 August, destroying its joinery department and a number of offices.

There was a similar pattern of raids in 1941, with the city escaping any

Air-raid precautions (ARP) warden in Norwich.
(Image courtesy of Norfolk County Council
Library and Information Service)

prolonged or sustained attacks. Never-theless, a further twenty-one citizens died and 104 were injured. Most raids were carried out by opportunistic single bombers taking advantage of heavy cloud cover to traverse the city and drop high explosive or incendiary bombs.

THE BAEDEKER BLITZ

As part of their campaign to destroy as much of the city as they could, the Luftwaffe began the aerial blitz of Norwich on 27 April 1942. A further raid was launched two nights later and followed up by major bombardments on 27 June and 2 August. The campaign left 258 locals dead and a further 784 with serious injuries.

Psychologically, the impact of the raids must have been particularly devas-tating for those living in Norwich, as the city had enjoyed a period of relative calm in the months prior to April. So much so, that many citizens had begun to ignore the air-raid sirens and calls to head for public or private shelters.

On the night of the first raid, up to thirty bombers began to unleash their payload on residential areas around the outskirts of the city, causing extensive and widespread damage. Before the bombs had fallen, the sky had been awash with parachute flares and the tracer fire of those RAF night-fighters that had been mobilised to counter the attack. Waves of high-explosive stick bombs were followed by a rain of incendiary shells which started a wild conflagration visible for many miles across Norfolk.

During the two hours of the raid, the German aircraft dropped 185 heavy bombs weighing in at over 50 tons each. Factories, shops and homes were destroyed or left burning and the official death toll was recorded as 162, with as many as 600 sustaining serious injuries. These casualties included brave individuals from the emergency services who lost their lives in the desperate struggle to cope with the onslaught and devastation caused by the sustained attack.

The follow-up raid, coming just two days later on Wednesday, 29 April, brought a further sixty-nine casu-alties and proved to be a much heavier – albeit shorter – attack in terms of its destruction of the city. It is possible that the loss of life was less than before, as almost all citizens responded to the air-raid sirens and headed for cover. This time, 112 high-explosive bombs and numerous incendiaries were dropped. In the early part of May, many of the victims were buried in public funerals held at Norwich cemetery.

Air-raid damage to Somerleyton Street in 1942. (George Plunkett)

Air-raid damage to St Andrews Broad Street. (Image courtesy of Norfolk County Council Library and Information Service)

THE CITY STRUGGLES TO RECOVER

Beyond the immediate impact of the Baedeker Blitz, the people of Norwich began to tackle the longer-term disruption. The loss of so many houses had left hundreds homeless, without any means of support, and more than 14,000 emergency ration cards had to be issued. Water mains had been put out of action and tons of debris and rubble had to be cleared to enable life to go on. It would be a slow recovery for a city rapidly coming to terms with the impact of total war.

Beyond the April raids, the Germans continued to attack Norwich throughout 1942, including a 'Fire Raid' in June during which three enemy aircraft were shot down. It was small comfort as the attack brought sixteen further deaths and destroyed a number of historic buildings. However, with more than a touch of good fortune, many of the city's landmark buildings survived, including the cathedral which had been bombarded with around 850 incendiary bombs but suffered only minor damage.

After 1942, the continuing German raids were on a comparatively small scale and during the last year and a half of the war, Norwich saw no further damage from enemy bombs.

THE BAEDEKER GUIDE

Karl Baedeker began publishing worldwide travel guides on 1 July 1827. At first these were produced in German, but when Karl died in 1859, his three sons – Ernst, Karl and Fritz – continued to run the business, producing the guides in other languages and establishing the name 'Baedeker' as synonymous with travel guides across the globe.

Written by specialists, each Baedeker guide contained a wealth of reference material including maps, routes, travel facilities and descriptions of important buildings, sights, attractions and museums. The first guides in English were produced by Karl Baedeker Junior.

In 1872, the business was relocated to Leipzig. In an ironic twist of fate, Allied bombers destroyed the headquarters and archives of the publishing house during the Second World War. The great grandson of Karl Baedeker later re-established the business that still operates to this day.

WAS IT ALL WORTH IT?

There is no doubt that the Baedeker Blitz of Norwich had a devastating and profound effect on the city and its inhabitants. Statistics produced after the war suggested that the April raids had required over £1 million to be spent on repair and recovery work alone. Some 358 dwellings had been totally destroyed and a further 1,678 were listed as 'not repairable'. Substantive repairs were subsequently made to nearly 25,000 houses.

Around eighty industrial establishments, offices, public buildings and business premises had also been totally destroyed, with many hundreds more being badly damaged and left in various states of repair. On top of that, the impact on Britain's defence resources has to be taken into account. Just one example will serve to illustrate the impact.

The Ministry of Works had to provide Norwich with squads of repair workers, including a peak of 500 in the month of May alone. To the end of that year, the average number of men employed in the aftermath of the blitz was calculated at 1,530 per day.

From a German point of view, the retaliatory bombing of the Baedeker raids had little to do with any military objectives and it would be hard to argue – as horrendous as the attacks were on individuals and communities – that the campaign had any strategic effect on the military campaigns of the Allied Powers or the general outcome of the war. In essence, they were instigated for domestic propaganda reasons to placate the German public and convince them that the Luftwaffe could strike at the heart of Britain – its culture and heritage – with relative impunity.

BIBLIOGRAPHY

PRINCIPAL PRIMARY SOURCES

Bury and Norwich Post
Illustrated London News
Ipswich Journal
Norfolk Chronicle
Report on the Collision which Occurred on 3rd February 1949, at Norwich, Trowse in the Eastern Region British Railways (His Majesty's Stationery Office, May 1949)
The Report of the Court of Inquiry Held in Pursuance of an Order of the Board of Trade … into the Circumstances Attending the Collision on the Great Eastern Railway on the 10th September 1874 (Her Majesty's Stationery Office, September 1874)
The Times

SECONDARY SOURCES

Brooks, Pamela, *Ghastly True Tales of the Norfolk Poisoners* (Halsgrove, 2007)
Chandler, Michael, *Murder & Crime in Norwich* (The History Press, 2010)
Emsley, John, *The Elements of Murder: A History of Poison* (Oxford University Press, 2005)
Meeres, Frank, *Norwich Murders & Misdemeanours* (Amberley Publishing, 2009)
Morson, Maurice, *Norwich Murders* (Wharncliffe Books, 2006)
Souhami, Diana, *Edith Cavell* (Quercus, 2011)
Storey, Neil R., *A Grim Almanac of Norfolk* (Sutton Publishing Ltd, 2003)

Printed in Great Britain
by Amazon